The Messenger

Des Ryan was born in 1952 in Geelong, Victoria, and having no say in the choice of birthplace, still supports the Geelong Football Club. For a time, he aspired to play on the wing for Geelong but had not the silky skills; he also thought of becoming a Christian Brother but he had not the ill-temper; and on leaving school he started an Applied Chemistry course but became quickly bored and dropped out. A serial failure seeking a good way to hide his intellectual shortcomings, he went into journalism. In his home town, he was considered good looking. A career in TV journalism beckoned. Once outside the confines of Geelong, however, doubts emerged about his looks and he went into radio. He worked at 3AW in Melbourne and 5DN in Adelaide, where he embraced the motto: 'If in doubt, cliché.' He had not the talent to read news bulletins on air but managed to remain in radio for much of the 1970s by mouthing the words. He discovered early that talkback radio did not amount to public opinion. In the eighties, he joined Messenger Newspapers. Observing the affairs of local government, Des soon realised the key to a long career was an attention to trivia, not to detail. He was made the editor. Needing someone to write a weekly column to challenge his own prejudices, he hired himself.

THE MESSENGER

DES RYAN

Selected Columns
from Messenger Newspapers,
Adelaide, 1993–2003

Wakefield
Press

Wakefield Press
1 The Parade West
Kent Town
South Australia 5067
www.wakefieldpress.com.au

First published 2003
Copyright © Des Ryan, 2003

Designed by Liz Nicholson, design BITE
Illustration by Jonathon Inverarity
Typeset by Clinton Ellicott, Wakefield Press
Printed and bound by Hyde Park Press

National Library of Australia
Cataloguing-in-publication entry

Ryan, Des.
The Messenger: selected columns from Messenger newspapers,
1993–2003.

ISBN 1 86254 613 4.

1. Newspapers – Sections, columns, etc. 2. Adelaide – Social
conditions. I. Title. II. Title: Messenger.

079.94231

Dedication

With thanks to Des Colquhoun, who set the standard.

Eternal optimism has no deadline

NO DOUBT about it, the opportunity to write a regular newspaper column such as the one I have been doing for Messenger Newspapers since 1993 is a rare treat. Ask anyone, and they will tell you how lucky I am, especially those who disagree with me and would like to see me punished for being contrary.

Being the Messenger editor possibly helped get me the gig, although, let it be noted, I have never received an extra payment for the additional worry. The editor is a hard man.

I never set out to be the Messenger columnist; the legendary Des Colquhoun was doing a fine job at the time he went on a South African safari for a month in September, 1993.

At a pinch, I filled in and the first column I wrote is also reprinted first in this selection, as well as the follow-up one, which pretty much wrote itself. One less column to worry about, I thought at the time.

Colquhoun returned in late October and continued writing his column until the end of the year. Then he announced his retirement, somewhat prematurely if you ask me.

At the start of 1994, I wrote a column thanking Colquhoun for his contribution, also reprinted here, while casting around for a replacement. I am still here, for good or ill.

In the early days, panicking, I remember having 14 columns up my sleeve at one stage in case I suffered writer's block. Now, I pretty much write as I go but the panic is always there hunched over my shoulder.

One thing the discipline of journalism teaches you is that when faced with a looming deadline and not a thought in your head, just sit there until something comes. Not the best thing for high blood pressure, however.

Some columns were dashed off quickly; others were agonised over; on average, though, each one took about three hours from the first thought on a blank screen to completion.

For those of us who learned to type on paper, I love the way computers are so forgiving in letting you constantly change your mind, and still can keep up.

Yes, computers are wonderful but notebooks are better. I carry one with me at all times and my friends have learned to be cautious in its presence. I have a pen and I know how to use it.

It took some convincing by Michael Bollen, of Wakefield Press, to make me bring together this selection in book form. I had always thought newspaper columns were intended to be read in their particular time and place, as dust on the wind, not to be contemplated many years later.

My first thought was to stick in just the pieces that had Adelaide as a theme; then I thought, well, some people liked The Duke years; others liked to read about my failing health; or the soft little parables; or the edgy social commentary; and almost everyone seemed to like seeing me embarrass myself. What the hell, you never can tell with readers.

Like Colquhoun, the day is coming when I, too, will be pensioned off and replaced by someone else. Did I say that or did I just think it?

My work here is not quite done yet.

Distilling the elusive essence of Adelaide

THE OTHER evening I was waiting for someone in Rundle Mall and the atmosphere was like a funeral where everyone was waiting for the corpse. The passersby, heads bowed into the rain and shoulders hunched, had that crumpled, humiliated look that comes to people who have been let down by someone they trusted.

The general effect was of people who had retreated into their shells to await ... what? The State election was my first guess.

Then I thought, if Adelaide were human, what sort of person would it be? What are we, collectively speaking, and what words do we use to explain ourselves to outsiders?

You can look at people's heavy-hearted faces in Rundle Mall and imagine who they are and what they do, and be wrong most of the time. But so far as a city is concerned, we are all passengers on the same time line, and it should be possible for us to reasonably define the character of a place.

All cities have different characters shaped by their geography, history, climate, easy access to vineyards and so on. Sydney, for example, is glitzy, crass, superficial and a great place to visit. I would not want to live there unless someone else paid for my absolute waterfrontage on the harbour.

Overseas travellers mostly recollect the places they visited not so much for the Eiffel Towers or Edinburgh Castles as for how well or ill-treated they were by the locals.

First-time visitors to Adelaide always remark on the clean, wide streets, the enormous quality of the sunlight and the quaint architectural one-offs drawn from nineteenth-century Europe. But that's the tourist stuff and too superficial to properly describe what I'm searching for. It does not identify that elusive quality about Adelaide that makes it unique – its spirituality, what energises it.

I have searched for this distilled essence over many lunches over many years, without success. I sometimes wonder if Adelaide's character lately has been sandpapered featureless by the constant erosion of hard times on soft people.

The problem remains: how can a place with such a wonderful lifestyle be so slippery to define? I don't know if it's possible to judge Adelaide in 25 words or less but people do it all the time about other places.

That's your challenge, dear reader, to come up with a telling observation about our City-State that manages to catch the flavour of the place, in 25 words or less starting with 'Adelaide is ...'

We'll print the best ones and I'll see if I can find a bottle of wine as a prize for the person whose defining words come closest to my heart.

29 September 1993

Adelaide and aunts: a match maiden heaven

WHAT IS IT about maidens, and about maiden aunts in particular, that makes people want to compare Adelaide to them? A maiden is a young unmarried girl, a virgin in all likelihood, and a maiden aunt is an older unmarried woman, a spinster, though not necessarily a virgin.

Yet the comparison of Adelaide to maidens and maiden aunts cropped-up time and again in our recent competition which asked readers to describe Adelaide. Among the dozens of entries were lots of endearing 'warm and fuzzies' about Adelaide, so many in fact that it seems there is little or nothing wrong with the place.

Many people, the majority as it happened, thought Adelaide conveyed a sense of 'home': safe, secure, reliable, trusting et cetera. It's good that so many people feel much love for this city although I am unsure that 'home' is such a strong marketing theme to attract tourists here. 'Adelaide – your home away from home' seems a trifle boring as a tourist slogan.

Colonel William Light got rave reviews from many people for designing such a lovely city. One person managed to find 26 words using the A to Z of the alphabet to describe Adelaide, although she stumbled a bit with the letter X for Xiting.

I was seriously concerned for Marion Mott, of Seaton: 'Adelaide is a mystery, the girl you love who breaks your heart. Baffling, angel and devil, highest and lowest of humankind struggle for victory here.' Ummm ... well, yes, I suppose so, Marion.

You can sense the betrayal that Laura Cunningham, of Christie Downs, feels about her Adelaide: 'Adelaide is a sweet maiden in soiled garments. Once she shone – tall and free. Now she cringes, retreating under the battery of thievery and rapine.' Whew!

Valerie Taylor, of Norwood, should have won this contest. Her polished contribution hit me with a sudden flash of recognition and made me smile. Sadly, at 48 words, it exceeded the 25 word limit and, sorry, Valerie, if there is one sure thing that can be said about Adelaide, rules are rules: 'Adelaide is a charming, genteel maiden aunt sitting primly in her Victorian drawing room – waiting. The door bursts open, admitting her teenage niece in a flurry of sunlight and fresh air. A slight frown creases Adelaide's brow. "Close the door, darling," she murmurs, "you're letting in a draught."'

But the winner is ... Kalyna Flowerpot of Kent Town, for this succinct effort: 'Adelaide is like an old-fashioned maiden aunt – kind, dependable, always well-presented, but a little dull if visited without company.'

Kalyna Flowerpot? Who knows? The fact that someone went to the trouble of submitting an entry, and then felt the need to use a made-up name, probably is a sharper commentary about Adelaide than anything else.

13 October 1993

Drinking in the legend of Des Colquhoun

JUST ABOUT everyone who knows Des Colquhoun has a favourite Colquhoun story. Mine is about the time he and a few mates were walking along King William Street past the GPO.

I cannot recollect whether they were on their way to the pub, or returning from it, but it was late at night and lying there sleeping on the pavement was a down-on-his-lucker, his shelf life practically expired.

'Lend me five dollars, will you?' Colquhoun asked of no one in particular among his mates. The five dollars was duly handed over, and Colquhoun slipped it fondly into the pocket of the derelict.

Colqhoun walked off, smiling to himself at the thought of the down-and-outer's surprised face when he awoke in the morning and checked his pockets. He would discover the five dollars and be disbelieving at first and then, probably for the first time in many years, he would sense that his luck had changed.

So what if he went and spent it on a cheap bottle of port or a packet of smokes? When you are that far down, even five dollars can make a big difference to your day and the moral tut-tutters can please themselves.

Colquhoun, the ministering angel in the night, understands this. He never bothers to size people up for their worth. He accepts everyone as he meets them, preferring to see the best in a person, never the worst, and to respect people without them ever having earned it.

Thanks for that, Desmond.

I first met him when he used to hold court in the dimly-lit old Marble Bar of the Ambassador's Hotel, still in King William Street. This was in the time before they ripped the guts out of the place and filled it with glass, brass and poker machines, and I doubt if Colquhoun has been back there since.

In the good old days, punctuating his stories with puffs of cigarette smoke, Colquhoun would embrace all comers, friends and strangers alike, in the warmth of his bonhomie. It was impossible ever to find him sitting alone in the Marble Bar, or anywhere else for that matter.

People would attempt to match him drink for drink and would end up slack-jawed, heads cocked to one side, trying to focus in one-eyed amazement as Colquhoun embraced yet another newcomer with his standard introductory one-liner: 'It's great to see you, buddy. Your buy!' I cannot say for sure that I have ever seen him drunk, or sober. It's hard to tell with Colquhoun.

Nowadays, he is not as well as he once was, although not dead. Colquhoun lives on in defiance of all medical wisdom and, indeed, will live forever.

But he has called it a day as Messenger's and Adelaide's pre-eminent newspaper columnist.

He claims, to quote him back to himself, that, 'I'm getting too scatty, doddery and remote to contribute to any effect. When you gotta go, you gotta go mate.'

For Christ's sake, Colquhoun, that's outrageous!

12 January 1994

Cold steel with pizza to follow

THESE WORDS are being written through gritted teeth for I had my annual colonoscopy this morning.

It's an ordeal, there is no other word for it. A rod of cold steel, no matter how dexterous the swordsman or how sedated the victim, is still a rod of cold steel and its purpose carries with it an undignified tale best left to the imagination.

Ordinarily, I avoid hospitals like the plague. They are dangerous places full of people in pain and, statistically speaking, the chances of you dying are higher there than anywhere else I can name right now. St Andrew's Hospital is not too bad, as far as hospitals go, and I know the ropes well enough now to be able to stroll into the place with an affected air of bored disinterest.

The same familiar aseptic smell, the nurses scurrying about and being their usual jolly selves, and the same blue-and-white striped surgical gowns, conveniently open-backed for just such a procedure as a colonoscopy.

Rebuilding work was under way on the first floor this morning and the corridor outside the day ward was alive with the noise of jackhammers, electric drills and the splitting crack of cold chisel on brick.

In the gaps between the demolition racket, agonised screams came from afar, perhaps from the maternity ward, or possibly from someone who had just got her bill. Whatever, the combination of the electric drill and the screams was having an unsettling effect on my feigned nonchalance.

Call me gutless if you like but if I had any guts left, would I be needing a colonoscopy? Tucked up in bed, idly wondering if I would be done first or last, I pretended to be dozing but was really sneaking furtive glances at my fellow colonoscopees.

There were four others: the older chap in the corner was staring disconsolately at the ceiling; the woman across from me smiled sheepishly when we made chance eye contact; and the two other women in the beds to my right had their faces hidden behind newspapers.

I was the last to be called, of course. The trouble with going last is you have to lie there and listen to the gentle sobbing of those who went before when they are brought back to the ward.

The chap in the corner was dead to the world, mouth agape and flat on his back in a pethidine dream, so one of the aides had to go up to him and yell in his ear: 'Excuse me, your wife rang to check that you are all right. Oh, yes, you look a bit better now – there is some colour coming back into your cheeks.'

The confused bugger spluttered and coughed and by the time he had come to his senses sufficiently to ask 'Waaa … waaa … what!!?', the aide had long gone.

I was discharged four hours after admission – not yet ready for the mortuary slab – and I retrieved my human nobility along with my clothes and had a sudden craving for seafood pizza after fasting for 24 hours.

Life goes on and all things come to pass, especially after a morning colonoscopy and a pizza for lunch. Better keep moving …

23 February 1994

Working magic on urbanised heart

IN THE EARLY daylight hours, the morning was an exceptional, faultless thing. Recent rain had wrought a miracle from the aridity, and ephemeral wildflowers blossomed across the plain and up the slopes of the Musgrave Ranges: colours of slubbed ochre and violet, mottled crimsons and rolled gold, with acacia trees pencilled along the skyline.

An eagle hovered on the thermals, spiralling higher and higher, and contemplated his chances of breakfast if we happened to run over a goanna or a snake.

Wally, the young Aborigine doing the driving, laughed hysterically every time the battered Toyota hit a pothole and we white fellas in the back crunched our heads against the roof.

The further we went into the Musgraves, trailing a plume of hanging red dust, the more I began to think of myself as looking back at my old self being left behind. This place was not my natural habitat but it had a wild, primal beauty that worked a magic on my urbanised heart: a clear-sighted understanding that less truly is more.

And a prickly sense that we city folk confuse our lives by following false trails and that life would be so much simpler were it not for other people.

This thought kept me occupied until, cracking our heads again, Wally gaily swerved toward a kangaroo that bounded off the road. 'Get you later!' he laughed out the window at the kangaroo, which perched on its haunches unconcerned.

'I'll have to take you blokes roo hunting,' Wally yelled over the noise of the wind in our ears. He said hunting kangaroos was easy. You just had to think like them.

'Yeah, full of hops,' muttered the old man sitting next to Wally – a Pitjantjatjara elder who was guiding us north of Ernabella to look at a rare waterfall that flowed spectacularly after heavy rain.

After lurching and ricocheting this way and that for half an hour, Wally parked the car in the shade of a ravine and we were enveloped in the smell of eucalypt and floral fragrances.

To get from there to the waterfall, the old fella said, we would have to leave the four-wheel drive and walk a distance up a fissure between the rocks.

I instinctively made sure the car door was locked before slamming it shut and then noticed the old man shaking his head. I knew immediately what was going through his mind: only a white city fella would be dumb enough to bother locking a car door way out here.

I gave him a sheepish grin and he said: 'Where they gonna take it, mate? Australia's a bloody island!'

9 March 1994

Throwing light on dark side of mall

REMEMBER when a shopping trip to the city was a special occasion for which people dressed up in their Sunday best – mum in her floral dress and the kids scrubbed and polished to within an inch of their lives?

Not any more, sad to say, although the other lunchtime I did spot one person in the city who was making a valiant, solo attempt to maintain the old dress standards.

Gossamered blond hair, lip gloss, blush, mascara, vivid green lurex dress, standing elegantly hand-on-hip at the corner of Angas and Pulteney streets – absolutely dazzling in the noonday sun. The scruffy sandshoes and five-day beard growth let him down badly but at least he made an effort.

What a pity, then, that what in the daytime looks innocuous and even beckoning, turns at night into a charm-less, threatening wasteland where no car passes and ordinary citizens feel afraid. I am speaking here of Rundle Mall after dark.

When the mall shuts down for the night, the shadowy kids in their stolen Nikes and death's head T-shirts move in to fill the black holes of alcoves and doorways. Being monstered by a fourteen-year-old girl and her girlfriends for a couple of dollars tends to take the shine off a soft, balmy evening stroll spent window shopping.

I don't mind them being there – why shouldn't they be? It's the way they snap at you from the shadows that gets my nerve ends fizzing.

Why aren't they on the sports field whacking each other with hockey sticks instead of loitering with discontent, whatever that means? Most threatening of all are not the abuse and surly remarks about being bald and fat, it is the silent sense of being watched by unseen, predatory eyes.

On the other hand, I never feel puny and vulnerable in Hindley Street or Rundle Street East, at either end of the mall, and it is no coincidence that both those places are brightly lit and filled with the rhythm of cars and people. The cafe society surging to the east; to the west, a more primal, hormonal surge altogether.

Yet, amid the dark fear of an unprovoked thumping, the tension in Rundle Mall catches at the back of my throat. To be left feeling so twitchy makes me angry.

This is Adelaide with a hard, raw edge to it; the heart of a city made heartless. Will the future really be like this?

Adelaide City Council is studying concept plans to make the mall awash with bright lights. Good, so far as it goes – maybe I will be able to identify the thug who mugs me.

What the mall really needs is people – perhaps a nightly hawker's market during the warmer months so that it becomes crowded with food stalls and movement.

On no account, not ever, should cars be banned from Hindley Street and Rundle Street East to turn them into pedestrian malls. Over my dead body, as they say – perhaps literally.

29 March 1994

Theatre role call

ABOUT TEN YEARS ago, I think it was, I was dragged one Saturday night to the Playhouse to see *Don Juan*, one of those costume revivals aimed at getting bums on seats to keep the accountants happy.

There was a real pig snuffling about in the dirt, stage front, and I can remember gangly Bruce Spence doing ridiculous flourishes with his sword. Until then, I had seen only two plays in my life: one was a repertory production of *The Pirates of Penzance*, which was terrible, and the other was *Jesus Christ Superstar*, which was okay but not as good as the record.

I now find that one of life's rare pleasures is to sit in a theatre and have the actors reveal something which I do not know, and sometimes what I don't want to know, about myself.

True, there has been some rubbish along the way, but I swore long ago I would never walk out on a play, no matter how appalling. As with wine, you can never really appreciate the good stuff until you have sampled the bad.

Except for musicals. You cannot get me to a musical by hook or by crook. I can never understand the words and the plot is generally as dull as ditchwater. There is an advertising adage that if the client's message is inane or the product execrable, then drag in the musos and turn it into a jingle. Andrew Lloyd-Webber has done rather nicely from it, thank you very much.

That apart, how remarkably pleasant it must be to stand up there on stage, live, and have the audience eating out of your hands – laughing, crying, whatever, all within spitting distance, literally.

My favourite Australian actor is Colin Friels. In the movie *Malcolm*, Friels was a harmless, warm-hearted simpleton whose obsession with trams led to hilarious escapades. To get me to laugh takes some doing, but Friels did it.

Two nights later, as it happened, I saw him at Her Majesty's in *Orphans*, alongside Warren Mitchell. Here Friels filled the stage as a raging, spitting, conniving hoodlum, struggling with his demons and, finally, pathetically vulnerable. The contrast was staggering. Friels wasn't just role playing – he had actually changed shape and substance, and he won me forever.

Meryl Streep never makes me suspend disbelief like that. To me, her characterisations are sprayed-on, not immersed. All I can see is her performing. Yes, she is technically good but in the end it's just clever Meryl up there going about her business and doing funny voices.

I once asked the State Theatre Company artistic director Chris Westwood what she liked most about actors. They're so trusting, she replied. So are dogs, but I think I know what she means.

What actors do is externalise for the rest of us the creative genius of the playwright and the director. The words are not the actors', their appearance is made up and even the place where they stand on the stage is specified.

When your career as an actor, your livelihood, everything, can go down the toilet at any time, it takes a very special kind of trust indeed to risk so much of yourself at the hands of others. No wonder actors are such vulnerable, insecure creatures.

13 April 1994

It's madness ...
but who cares?

IT IS NOT as if I have personal experience in the field of mental illness although there are days when I have to wonder about my own sanity. Days when I can think of nothing better than to be hidden away for a while behind a walled garden. Solitude is bearable, even reinvigorating, if it is freely chosen.

Semaphore is no walled garden. A one-legged man sits naked in a wheelchair on Semaphore Road footpath; another repeatedly criss-crosses the street speaking into a walkie-talkie with a five-metre aerial; a bald man in a frock carries a string bag filled with odd socks.

These people, of course, have as much right to be on the streets as anyone else and they might even have discovered the meaning of life. Sanity is such a marginal state of mind, anyway.

They are just like you and me except they have a few problems that need treatment, that's all.

Take the middle-aged man sitting in the bus shelter on Woolnough Road. It was raining and there was no sun, yet he shielded his eyes as soon as I stood there under cover with him, in a gesture of, I cannot see you, so you cannot see me.

He was sitting there nervously kicking the side of the shelter with a sandal, mumbling to himself about my unwelcome presence, and gingerly touching a lump on the side of his face. He wore no socks and his ankles were swollen; after a time, he arose awkwardly from the bench. But his legs were gone and he had to sit down again.

I asked him if he was okay and he was silent, as if thinking for a moment before he came up with the answer. There was no answer, only silence, and he began to gouge at the corners of his eyes with his thumbs.

Suddenly he blurted out 'All my teeth are my own!' and opened his mouth wide. There were only four of them and they were bad.

Then he cleared his throat: 'The bus is coming!' There was no sign of it. When a bus did come a few minutes later, he said: 'Hold my horse!' Then off he hobbled across Semaphore Road.

He has not much of a life. My life is not all it should be either but that is a lifestyle problem; I still have free choices.

Abandoned to the streets, victims of circumstances beyond their control, is it asking too much to expect the government to ensure these hostel outcasts get proper care?

Or have we become so damned careful not to discriminate against them, with their behaviour problems and their alcohol problems and their suicide problems, that they are being left without the treatment they need, a danger to themselves?

Is this hazy notion of removing discrimination really economic rationalism under the guise of concerned welfare? Deinstitutionalisation is a word that only an economist could love.

The next time you see someone urinating in the gutter, ask yourself this: Is he crazy or is he just making a social comment?

29 March 1995

It's Little Mikey and the big bad racists

HOW DID little Mikey Brander get to be the leader of the racist gang National Action?

Did he beat all the other, bigger NA chaps in a peeing contest or something? It is hard to imagine how you can piddle higher than everyone else if you sit down to take a pee.

There must be a simple explanation. Perhaps he is on steroids. Growth hormones can make you edgy and irritable. And why does he look so miserable all the time? Do you have regular bowel movements at the same time every morning, Mikey?

Or perhaps you are taking your medication in the wrong order. I honestly don't know if you're on anything, Mikey, but it's time you had a urine test.

For a leader, he always looks the odd one out alongside the other chaps, doesn't he? So neat, so tidy, so freshly-scrubbed. So very white.

The bigger lads really should do something about their personal hygiene and dress standards if their intention is to panic the populace by frightening them.

Frankly, chaps, the old shaved heads, mirrored sunnies, grunge T-shirts, bovver boots and beer guts have become rather ho-hum. Imagine if you were out there in bell-bottom trousers and pink paisley shirts with stringray collars? Now that is a truly frightening thought.

You could even work up a baton-twirling routine among yourselves, with Mikey out front doing the splits in a delicious green leotard. With a 'Have a nice day' button pinned to his chest, screaming 'I hate Asians!' Terrifying.

Selecting the right music might be a problem. The chaps look like they're into heavy metal but try telling me Mikey isn't a Partridge Family fan.

When they take to the streets, Mikey and the bigger chaps always remind me of a male mutual support group who have managed to give their escorts the slip on a weekend excursion.

Hey, loosen up, guys! Even political revolutionaries with a brittle potential for violence can still get in touch with the inner child. Follow your leader.

Little Mikey seems to be afflicted by his own brand of attention deficit disorder: 'Look at me, everybody – look at me, me, me!' Afterwards, I imagine him going home to be greeted with 'Little man, my what a busy day you've had,' and have his mum tuck him into bed with a hot mug of Horlick's. Or perhaps he gets a whack over the head for mixing with the wrong company.

Was he an annoying little brat as a kid or is he just an annoying little brat now? This is a fair question since he has made such a public spectacle of himself with his anti-Asian street marches and by standing for election to Enfield Council on Saturday week.

There are other questions. What does he do for a living? What does he want out of life, personally speaking? Does he have any distinguishing birthmarks or tattoos? Does he eat Chinese takeaway? Does he drive a Japanese car? Does he varnish his toenails? C'mon, Mikey, get a life.

26 April 1995

SA going all the way – in what direction?

IN MY EARLY DAYS here, twenty or more years ago, whenever the locals were asked what they liked most about Adelaide, they put big quote marks around the word with their fingers every time they spoke it: 'Lifestyle'.

Quite right, too. Adelaide was a big country town where people had the ability to relax with outsiders and to make them relaxed in return.

I thought they were the most hospitable people in the land; a trifle smug, perhaps, but then who could blame them? This, need I say it, was before the State Bank collapsed while no one was watching.

To my mind, Adelaide was a girl with a pleasant, sweet disposition, and a better class of vowel, the sort of lover you could take home to meet your wife.

Adelaide was never what you might call wild or impulsive. Truth be told, the only hint of unpredictability would be if the weather failed to turn out as expected.

It was a gentle, ordered and homely society, a creature of fixed habits and customs. It was also a tolerant society that disliked extremism in all its forms and which showed tolerance to people who did not deserve it, and still does.

So what, may I ask, has happened to Adelaide's customary cheeriness? Look at the way we behaved when we lost the Grand Prix to Victoria. Did we whinge, did we mope around afterwards feeling hard done by? You bet we did! We booed and whistled from the safety of our side of the border, sullen and resentful, feeling sorry for ourselves.

There was bad blood between neighbours and hollow threats, as if the Vics were going to take pity on us and change their minds. We might as well have been conversing with the office water cooler for all the difference it made. And deep down we knew we deserved to lose the Grand Prix because we did not understand the value of what we had until it was too late. How very Adelaide.

Since then, it has been just one damn thing after another, hasn't it? The Crows are hopeless, we lost the State of Origin footy and we cannot win the Sheffield Shield to save ourselves.

We are so far down we are starting to make jokes at our own expense. 'Adelaide is the original good time girl that was had by everyone else.' The public mood is one of gloomy analysis, miserable navel gazing and chronic negativity. All our windows of opportunity are covered in dark security mesh. Don't you just hate the 90s?

The new 'Going All The Way' slogan for our number plates – adopted by State Cabinet obviously without first seeking the feedback of Ministers' wives – is supposed to capture the mood of pride in ourselves that is thought to be there just below the surface. Terrific, if it works.

The last time I went all the way, I fell asleep on the last bus from the city and woke up locked inside the Elizabeth bus depot. It can happen if you take the wrong route home.

2 August 1995

Sunday, bloody Sunday, bliss

THIS MUCH I KNOW: soft Sunday mornings spent reading the papers or a good book, shared with a close companion and a short-black coffee, is a reminder that all is right with the world.

Luxuriating in dappled light through the vines, surrounded by soft air and space where even the darkest shadow is transparent, and to be aware of the power of silence, of the slightest breath or movement in your partner. Not snoring, just purring.

To sit together as if the other is not there, a sense of mood, feeling no pressure to fill the space with chitchat. Smiling at a shared intimacy where affection and companionship are more important than sex. And to savour syrupy Greek coffee or, at a pinch, espresso – demitasse, the stronger the better.

The book I am reading is *A Good Life* by Ben Bradlee, the former editor of the *Washington Post* during the Watergate years. It should be subtitled *If I Sat On Wet Grass, My Pants Would Rust*, the tinny bugger.

Bradlee reports that while on a drinking binge in Sydney as a US naval ensign in World War II, he ran across a group of Australian soldiers who were home for the first time in five years after fighting in Crete, North Africa and New Guinea.

Although Bradlee himself had been in the war all of five minutes, he already was well on the way to wearing a decorative chestful of fruit salad.

In contrast, he noted, the Australians, even after all their wartime campaigns, wore no decorations whatever, 'other than the curved metal AUSTRALIA at the top of their shoulders'.

I felt a jolt of pride when I read that, an accolade to our best characteristics without pomposity or overblown boasts. I have an instinctive liking for the laconic wit of people who can prick the inflated egos of others with: 'Got any spare tickets on you, mate?' Even when it is directed against me.

Are we still the same people 50 years later? Sitting here relaxed under the vine, the answer is yes, the same.

Different in some respects – the spice rack of multiculturalism, to name a good one – but still the same when it comes to the things that matter: understated, wry good humour and defence of the underdog. May it forever remain so.

Believe it or not, the military is supposed to have a secret plan for dealing with civil insurrection. I find it hard to imagine the circumstances under which such an uprising could occur in Australia, or that the military would be overly bothered about it.

At least not on a Sunday morning.

17 January 1996

Left cold by the summer's heat

SNOW IS AS RARE on the ground in Adelaide as rocking-horse manure, more's the pity, but here is a pleasant thought to help tide you over the worst of the summer heat: If your car becomes stranded in a snow drift during a blizzard, what two survival items are necessary to keep you alive through the night?

A candle, is the first answer. Canadian motorists always keep one in the glovebox since the heat generated by a single candle is said to be enough to prevent a person from freezing to death. Presumably, the candle would need to be a long one and not a birthday cake candle.

I cannot recollect the last time I drove into a snow drift in Adelaide, certainly not at this time of the year. A saline drip would be more advisable than a candle.

Adelaide has too much summer for my liking. I seem to spend all my time squinting and hyperventilating and my digestive system gives up the ghost and I get into heated domestic disputes. My wife has reptilian blood and is only ever really comfortable on the hottest of summer days.

For me, summer must be endured bad humouredly, day upon infernal day, especially when the expected two-day heatwave turns into two weeks and life is not worth living.

We argue. My line is, you can take off only so many clothes before you are charged with public indecency and you will still be hot. In winter, on the other hand, you can always wear fleecy lined underwear and rug-up and be perfectly comfortable.

The one saving grace about Adelaide's summer is that at

least it is a dry heat. I once went to Darwin in the pre-Wet and could feel myself rotting from the inside and I have no intention of ever returning to that tropical hell hole.

Now, I have nothing in particular against the Weather Bureau and I suppose its weather forecasts are as correct as its ability to make them so. Nor do I expect the Bureau to be able to exert its influence on the weather.

At the same time, I think it is perfectly reasonable to expect it to be accurate in the matter of predicting cool changes. Its track record is pretty abysmal in this regard, let me tell you, as cool changes are all I live for in Adelaide's summer. Every time the Bureau promises a change that never arrives, its staff should be held to account by having their air conditioning turned off.

That aside, summer here is boring and dull, day after endless day of blazing sun when nothing moves except the heat haze. If we are going to have weather then at least it should be interesting, with plenty of rain and wind.

And another thing: Stout in summer is undrinkable, no matter how chilled it is. I like stout.

I am interested to know what the weather was like on Proclamation Day in December 1836, when Governor Hindmarsh stood under the Old Gum Tree in his heavy, buttoned-up uniform.

Personally, were it thirty degrees or more, I would have climbed back aboard the *Buffalo* and headed for Canada instead.

What else do you need to survive in a Canadian snow-drift? A box of matches.

31 January 1996

An X-ray vision of Adelaide's soul

YES, I AM BACK, and just take a look – Oi! – so where do you think you are off to? Come back here at once, sit down and behave!

Now, take a look at these calf muscles, like Christmas hams. Now the feet, tough as tanned leather – and the gout is much better, too, thank you. Such are the side benefits of backpacking the northern hemisphere on a shoestring.

You will doubtless be pleased to know my health has been good, not counting an attack of the diabolicals in Spain that left me tearfully bidding farewell to an excellent lunch of pig's ear, chorizo sausage and black pudding. I have lost weight but it won't last, sadly.

An aside. Just before departing, I bumped into a former colleague of mine, David X, who had returned to Adelaide after twenty months abroad.

Over a drink, which I had to buy, X said that after travelling through Southeast Asia, the Indian subcontinent and the Middle East, the only word he could think of to describe Adelaide on his return was 'weird'. This, from a man who thought Syria was the happiest, friendliest place he had visited. The word 'weird' needed to be considered in that context.

He said it was difficult to pinpoint precisely what he meant by weird but the people on the streets of Adelaide had an air of – I interrupted him with my own suggestions: Despondency? Sullenness? Resentment?

No, X said, chewing his moustache thoughtfully, there was simply nothing showing in their faces, nothing at all. It reminded him of a melancholy dream sequence in which he is walking along a street with streams of blank-faced automatons coming the other way, and no matter what he does to attract their attention, they walk by without noticing him.

I do not find this very surprising given the effect X can have on people. I, too, have sometimes averted my gaze trying to ignore him on the street, though never with much success.

He got me thinking, however, as his observation ran counter to my view that Adelaideans are appreciative of anyone interested enough in them to come visit. I slotted X's thought away as a minor pebble flicked into a puddle.

Now, having just returned from overseas myself, all I can say, X, is bollocks! To fly back home from a soggy, crowded and noisy Europe to see the way Adelaide absorbs the sunlight and radiates it back again in its own golden glow, to luxuriate in the enormous vacant spaces, to not be deliberately run down by crazed taxi drivers and, yes, to see genuinely friendly faces and to experience simple human courtesies again – these, X, are the powerful images of Adelaide. And I am supposed to be a cynic.

Soon after returning, I was sitting by myself at dawn on the front verandah of a borrowed shack across the Gulf, watching sunrays spear from behind the Adelaide Hills on the horizon. It was the stuff of paradise and to the rest of an immensely crowded world, it would be.

We take Adelaide for granted, which we are entitled to do, I suppose, since it is ours, but in this clear and radiant morning, I was thinking the place where we live offers incomparable opportunities and it is about time we got on with them.

8 January 1997

Don't be fooled by appearances

ON THE WALL behind the altar in the Yankalilla Anglican church is a crinkled piece of plasterwork which is supposed to be a miracle apparition of the Blessed Virgin.

Yes, and if you lie on your back in the fields nearby and look at the clouds, you can see an elephant, the Last Supper and Gary Ablett going for a screamer, all in the same afternoon.

Now, I am unwilling to state categorically that it is not the BV, although what she is doing on the wall of an Anglican church, and not a Catholic one, is beyond me.

The explanation being put around by the entrepreneurial local priest, a certain Father Michael Nutter, is that Mary MacKillop, one of whose ubiquitous school houses is not far away, would likely have prayed in his church last century.

The MacKillop woman, as everyone knows by know, needs a third miracle to have her ranking raised from Blessed to Saintly by the Catholic Church. The faithful are expectant.

On one wall, dozens of small white cards have been attached to a pinboard, each containing a hand-written description of an ailment which requires a miracle cure. 'Aura – lung cancer', for instance. The cards are poignant in their simplicity.

Others list the sad ailments of our times and it is hard to know precisely what the BV is expected to do about them. 'Dad – to become a Christian and stop swearing'; 'Ray – chronic depression'; 'Suzanne – anxiety'; 'Emmanuelle –

fears'; 'Stephanie – stop smoking'; 'Anthony – choking on baby food'; 'Pete – wrongly accused'. Poor Pete. There also is a 'Fr Michael – tiredness'. Surely not you, Father Michael Nutter! At least he has a sense of humour.

One thing intrigues me: Why does the BV insist on appearing at such out of the way places? Take Fatima, for example, the remote shrine of pilgrimage in Portugal, not the Turkish belly dancer. Fatima is where three shepherd children had visions of the BV in 1916. She made five appearances from May through to October, which, by happy convenience, coincides with the summer tourist season.

She also popped up at three separate locations. Perhaps her transporter beam was out of whack and this may explain why she has now turned up at Yankalilla and not in Rundle Mall, as she no doubt intended. The Lord moves in mysterious ways and so does the Blessed Virgin, apparently.

No one is saying the Yankalilla apparition is really just a shoddy piece of plasterwork. The plasterer is reportedly threatening to sue and it is probably wiser and potentially very profitable to believe in miracles rather than to be dragged through the courts.

A spring of water has since bubbled from the ground near the church and Father Nutter is selling it to the pilgrims. The spring may be the BV's doing or, on the other hand, it might be where Tjilbruke shed more of his tears in Aboriginal Dreaming.

One myth at a time is all I can cope with.

15 January 1997

When SP bookies were the best bet

RONNIE THE RAT ran a highly successful SP bookie operation from home until the police raided him and he could not explain what fourteen phones were doing in his attic. The police dubbed him Rooftop Ron.

The story, as told by Ronald himself, particularly affected me when I first heard it at The Duke of Brunswick Hotel. He now sells insurance. This affected me almost as much.

As you can imagine, Ronald's wife, Gwen, was not well pleased when she returned home to discover that every door from the front to the attic had been banged off its hinges by The Plod. She left Ronald to await collection at the City Watch House longer than was strictly necessary – but knowing Gwen, she had probably opened a bottle of top-notch champagne and was having a good grin.

Ronald is a dapper little chap with a moustache, immaculately dressed in a blue reefer jacket and a colourful line of ties, who reminds me of, well, an SP bookie. I make a point of calling him Ronald instead of Rat, as just about everyone else does, as a mark of respect for a man who lived life on the edge and got caught red handed, no excuses.

Ronald was fined $10,000 for his sins, suffered some collateral damage from the Taxation Department and was forbidden from entering any South Australian race track.

Mind you, hardly anyone else goes to the races either these days and it occurs to me that race crowds went into decline around the same time as Ronald was being put out to pasture. The raid happened in the 1980s and it must have been one of the last big police operations of its type.

Under the combined weight of the TAB and Sky Channel and betting in pubs, the market was suddenly awash in legitimate betting outlets, and the SP bookie simply slammed his bags and moved on. Supply and demand, far more than any police crackdown, put paid to the business.

Ronald thinks there might be one retired SP who still takes a few bets for a couple of hours on a Saturday morning for old time's sake. Other than that, he knows of no SP bookies operating in South Australia.

A great pity, really. Although I rarely bet, except on the Melbourne Cup and when The Duke's horse Pantala is running, I remember with nostalgia those rainy afternoons spent in the pub watching the furtive bloke in the trilby ringing through the bets to someone such as Ronald.

It was a culture all of its own, populated by colourful characters just like Ronald, short of stature but larger than life. There were always rumours of imminent police raids, suspicions about why one SP got turned over but not another, and more than one young lad went on to a successful legal career after acting as an SP lookout in case the police turned up unexpectedly.

In fact, it was all terrific fun, one of those crimes with a highly reliable level of customer service in which no one was hurt unless you count the State Treasury as a helpless victim, and not many people do.

For my money, it beat the hell out of watching people moronically punch buttons on a pokie machine. And the payout was better.

As Ronald puts it: 'Desmond, it is the beginning of the end and my taxi is waiting.'

2 April 1997

Circus Boy's roots still in evidence

'NEVER TRUST a bear.' You simply cannot buy that kind of advice nowadays, can you?

It is the sort of tip that Anton Gasser, of Silver's Circus, drops matter-of-factly into the conversation as if everyone needs a working knowledge of bears.

Bears cannot be trusted, Anton warns. One minute they will be all playful and licking you and the next they will bite your head off, just like that. Wisely, Anton does not have bears at Silver's.

What he does have are three female lions, two camels – Salami and Humphrey – three llamas and, believe it or not, two Scottish Highland cattle. Anton says the cattle are highly intelligent. They are made to trot around the circus ring – which, given their natural inclination to do nothing whatever, I suppose is a feat in itself.

Anton is an old mate of David 'Circus Boy' Black, an Adelaide lawyer who spent four years with the circus in between sitting for his law exams in the early 1970s.

Blackie did his fair share of clowning – still does – but his real specialty was to be able to spin plates while standing atop a couple of balance balls. He boasts he was the best plate spinner in Australia. Hardly a crowded field, you would have thought, but no doubt it was good training for a legal career.

The word that springs to mind to describe Blackie is mercurial, in the sense that he is restlessly quick-witted and unable to stand still for more than ten seconds. The word that does not spring to mind is forceful.

Once, when he was with Anton's circus in Port Augusta, a gang of bikies tried to gatecrash the Big Top during the camel performance. The camel handler, keen to join the ensuing fight, handed Circus Boy his whip and, as Blackie says, the camels took one look at him, quickly sized up the situation, then sprinted from the tent and kept going.

Somewhere in the Outback there are two camels wearing striking blue silk canopies over their humps.

Anton tells another story about how Blackie, by now a practising lawyer and a bit under the weather, turned up during showtime shouting hello to all his old mates, tripped over the circus ring and fell flat on his face in the sawdust.

The audience, thinking it was part of the act, went wild. Once a clown, always a clown. Circus Boy claims not to remember the episode, which is possibly true.

People do not run away to join the circus any more. The work is too hard and only family dynasties, which circuses have always been, can be bothered with it.

But standing there alongside Anton – in the sawdust, under the Big Top – Blackie's eyes glazed over nostalgically. Who needs to be a lawyer when you are the best plate spinner in Australia?

21 May 1997

Afraid of jumping?
No fear!

LAST SATURDAY MORNING, with nothing better to do, I went to Strathalbyn and jumped from a plane at 12,000 feet for the first time.

Got your attention now? A couple of weeks earlier, I wrote a piece about how I had eaten my first pie floater and survived, which left only a parachute jump as the ultimate challenge in life. So Skydive Adelaide, a club with a keen eye for self promotion and a perverse sense of humour, invited me to make a tandem jump. I really must be more careful with what I write.

My instructor's name was Ralph. As you might expect of a man who had done 4600 previous jumps, Ralph was a doer not a talker.

'Breathe normally – if you have trouble breathing, it's because you're not,' he told me, then warned: 'I'll be too busy during the freefall to talk.'

Perhaps he feared I was going to interview him and take notes on the way down.

'It's like riding a motorbike flat out,' he explained. Having never ridden a motorbike either, the comparison meant nothing to me.

Ralph squeezed me into a tight-fitting jump suit which made me look for all the world like a large black condom, then buckled on a harness and we did a ground rehearsal of what would happen in the air. I began to like Ralph's quiet, disciplined manner as he went through the checks.

I mean, the last thing you want to hear is: 'Groan, I've got a hangover this morning like you wouldn't believe.' Skydive

Adelaide is strict about the consumption of alcohol – while sensible, this makes me wonder if it is really the sport for me.

Connected at the hips and shoulders, I felt a growing attachment to Ralph. Which is just as well since the required jumping position is rather too close to a graphic depiction in the Kama Sutra for my liking, rather like playing spoons in bed.

It means placing a helluva lot of trust in someone you have only just met.

Fifteen minutes later, squashed into a little plane with my left foot going to sleep, I was surrounded by eight other Skydive members, mostly young men, whose helmets bore such slogans as: 'No Fear'.

In my day, the term 'no fear' meant something altogether different, as in: 'Would you jump out of a plane?' 'No fear, I wouldn't.'

A couple of times on the way up, Ralph checked to see if I was going to faint, throw up or chicken out. 'No Fear!' I shouted, but he apparently didn't hear me over the noise of the plane.

Finally, after a twenty-five-minute climb above the clouds, squatting there with your toes over the edge of the open hatch, the Point of Balance becomes the Moment of Truth becomes the Point of No Return and the next you know, you are Out There.

Next week: The Jump.

28 May 1997

Plummeting to new heights

AFTER JUMPING from a plane at 12,000 feet, it takes about a week to come down to earth. Exhilarating is one word for it; I cannot think of any other context except for skydiving where I might use the word. Bloody exhilarating.

Ralph, the Skydive Adelaide tandem master with whom I recently leaped over Strathalbyn, still gets an adrenalin high even after 4600 jumps. Some days he does ten jumps and it makes me wonder if he bothers with a sex life.

I hesitate to take a rise out of Ralph, however. I trusted him with my life and having plummeted towards earth attached together at 200 km/h, you might say I have, ahem, fallen for him.

We had a couple of false starts, Ralph and I. Squatting in the open hatch, with me in front, twice I began to lean out prematurely, thinking we were on our way, only to be pulled back by Ralph, whose feet were not yet in the correct position.

The delay gave me time to think. There is something about standing on the edge that makes you ask yourself if you are completely mad, a split second of doubt. Then you are out there.

I did what Ralph had instructed me to do – arched back, hips thrust forward, arms held just so – and we performed a quick clockwise spin at one point; I assume Ralph did the spin on purpose. Or perhaps I raised the wrong eyebrow.

At that height, were it not for the rush of the wind and the madly flapping cheeks, you might just as easily be floating. The clouds were far, far below; next we dived into them, a soft, silent, wet world; then the 'chute opened.

Ralph gave me a couple of parachute straps to hold onto and invited me to stand on his feet to raise myself up and relieve the pressure of the harness digging into my groin. Everything still seems to be in the correct place, more or less.

It took four or five minutes: 45 seconds to freefall the first 7000 feet (do your own metric conversion – the old measure sounds more impressive to me) and the rest of the time was spent gently floating to the ground.

Exhilarating! But the experience of free-falling is as nothing compared to the fact of actually having done it.

Two hours later, there I was doing the week's supermarket shopping, back to earth with a jolt, and as I trolley-jostled my way around the aisles I could not help but affect a superior air. I mean, ha-ha, how many other shoppers had jumped from a plane at 12,000 feet that morning?

For days afterwards, still high as a kite, I buttonholed anyone who would listen to retell my tale of derringdo. I became boring. I didn't care.

Astonishing. Having survived two death-defying feats in the same month – eating a pie floater and jumping from a plane – I appear to be still alive.

Whatever next? Is there nothing else to live for? And will I ever get through this latest midlife crisis?

4 June 1997

The Duke's cycle of depression goes on

KIEREN, THE PUBLICAN at The Duke, goes by various nicknames including The Publican but the one that sticks is Big Fella, in the sense that he is large enough to kickstart a jumbo jet.

Motorbikes are another matter, however.

As a farm boy from Wudinna, on the Eyre Peninsula, it goes without saying that The Big Fella must have kickstarted a motorbike hundreds, even thousands, of times.

He recently went back to Wudinna for a relaxing week with the rellies on the farm, putting up sheds, erecting fences and having a ticketyboo time doing what the rest of us city folk would regard as bloody hard yakka and not a holiday at all. You can take the boy out of the country but you cannot take the country out of the boy.

And, of course, there were motorbikes to be ridden, the whole shebang, and on the weekend before he was due to return to The Duke, The Big Fella hopped on a bike, as he had been doing all week, and gave it a kick.

It did not start the first time, so he decided to give it a really big go and drove the kickstart bolt through his right calf behind the shin bone and out the other side.

The Big Fella is a good Catholic, as straight as they come, and were he not still under sedation in hospital at the time of writing this, I would ask him if he cursed and swore and took the Lord's name in vain. I know I would.

He spent two and a half hours lying under a tree with the bike still on top of him while the relatives mopped his brow and a doctor at Ceduna gave instructions over the telephone to a young nurse about how much morphine she should administer to someone of The Big Fella's size.

The accident happened at around nine in the morning. By the time the local CFS had done its bit and the air ambulance had flown him back to Adelaide, by my calculation, ten hours had elapsed before The Big Fella was finally operated on, the entire time spent with the bolt still sticking through his leg.

Now the blokes at Wudinna want him to send back the bolt so they can get the motorbike started.

The Big Fella was lucky, to the extent that anyone can count himself lucky with a bolt sticking through his leg. Lucky it did not smash the shin bone, lucky that his jeans plugged the hole as the bolt went through so he didn't bleed, and lucky a nurse happened to be at Wudinna.

It has been a less than happy year so far at The Duke, with one drama and another. A couple of people have died, others have been diagnosed with various ailments, and now The Big Fella.

While none of these has actually occurred on the premises, there is now talk of adapting the EFTPOS machine in the lounge bar to take Medicare cards.

The place is overdue for a touch of the crucifix and a sprinkle of holy water. You cannot beat a good, old fashioned exorcism.

18 June 1997

Close brush with hairafter

WHEN I HAD a full head of hair as a kid, I almost needed a general anaesthetic to make me have a haircut. Now that I am practically bald, I can hardly wait until the next time to hear what Merilyn has in store for me.

Merilyn is the local barber. She gives me a Number One and tries to charge me the pensioner rate, for which I forgive her, and we have interesting chats, *veeery* interesting chats, as it happens.

In the early days it was just small talk, such as the best places to eat and why it always looked as if she had done her own hair with a hand grenade.

Later on, we began to discuss issues such as the meaning of life, as one does. I was sitting there this afternoon and Merilyn said I was looking a bit flat, and I said that was funny because I felt perfectly fine until walked into her shop and, yes, I did feel flat all of a sudden.

I jokingly suggested she should get the feng shui man in to rid the place of its bad spirits and she said, well, as a matter of fact, she had Chinese chimes hanging outside the back door for precisely that reason.

I eyed her in the mirror, a picture of sartorial negligence, and wondered if she had been sniffing too much of her own hairspray. Now, Merilyn is neither bizarre nor eccentric in the ordinary sense but when she started talking about the 'presence' in her shop I thought she was extracting the urine.

She went on to say it was a benign presence, as if seeking to reassure me, and said her life was surrounded by the smell of incense, a good sign because it meant the spirits were looking after her. Uh-huh, and mine is surrounded by the whiff of sulphur.

She said she had taken up meditation, which gave her a higher high than drugs or drink, and she was gradually becoming aware of her psychic powers.

I felt my upper lip curling into a sneer but I put on the best blank face I could manage in the circumstances. If you insist, Merilyn, if you insist, keeping a watchful eye on the cut-throat razor in her hand.

As proof of her new-found powers, she told me how a customer recently came into the shop and, without him needing to announce it, she immediately knew about the birth of a grandchild and even knew the child's name.

My eyelids must have flickered because Merilyn gave me a smile as cold as a centrefold's and warned me not to print any of this because her mother would read it and think she was crazy. Good for you, Mum.

Who knows what other revelations Merilyn has in mind the next time I visit? I hope it is something useful like revealing the whereabouts of my missing sunglasses.

25 June 1997

Hanging out with the big knobs

The Mars Bar and the Adelaide Club have nothing whatever in common, one being a gay bar in Gouger Street and the other the final word in the rarefied atmosphere of private clubland on North Terrace.

They do not have reciprocal membership rights, of that I am fairly certain. Yet there I was last week in both places, one an invitation to lunch, the other one of those late night half-dares that seemed like a good idea at the time. Figure out for yourself which was which.

They have their differences. When you offer your hand at the Adelaide Club, someone shakes it; at the Mars Bar, they stamp ink on it. The Mars Bar also has lots of men openly kissing each other; I did not notice anything like this at the club. On the walls of the Mars Bar are photographs of muscular males with their shirts off, in the style of Robert Maplethorpe; at the Adelaide Club, the walls are covered with original paintings: Streeton, Heysen and so on.

In the club foyer hangs an honour board of members who lost their lives during World War II. There are just four names, which seems a fortunately low number of casualties. I expect the club had more casualties among the Lloyd's Names of investors who lost their money in bad insurance investments.

There is no honour board of any description in the Mars Bar unless you count the graffiti in the toilet. If you stand there having a pee in the Mars Bar urinal, the chaps on either side quite openly check out your equipment. I suppose this saves time later.

At the Adelaide Club, the urinals are those semi-enclosed, individual porcelain units which afford a degree of modesty and some protection against splashing your boots.

Each Mars Bar cubicle contains a sharps box attached to the wall above the cistern for the disposal of used syringes. There are no sharps boxes in the cubicles at the Adelaide Club.

What the club offers, however, are two whips hanging on the toilet wall. Each has a polished, wooden grip about the size of a feather duster's handle but instead of feathers, there are lengths of green leather, frayed at the ends.

They were too short to be of any use as mops and in the absence of a better explanation, the possibility of them being flagellation whips was enough to keep me amused for the time being. Disappointingly, I later discovered they were used by the members to polish their shoes without having to bend over.

In order to get inside the Adelaide Club, the one stipulation was I could name no names afterwards, which was fair enough since it was a private club and I had no wish to embarrass my host, this time. Nor would he allow me to steal a copy of the club membership list, which I thought was being overly pernickety. After all, I am a journalist – trust me.

Before I left the Adelaide Club, I found a copy of my old book *It's Grossly Improper* on a shelf in the library room and signed and dated it as proof that I was there, if only once. The book sits there, I do not. Curious.

Being neither gay nor clubbable, I guess both places are not meant for the likes of me. Give me a cubicle with a secure lock on it and I am happy.

16 July 1997

The Messenger

Duke goes to blazes despite holy spirits

DO NOT EVEN ASK me what the Christian Fellowship was doing at The Duke last night. All I know is that a pub is not the place to hold a prayer meeting and no wonder it caught fire.

By the time I turned up, flames were shooting out the chimney and there were more flashing lights than the brewery's Christmas display: fire trucks, a police roadblock and an ambulance standing by just in case.

The accusing fingers all were pointed at Stazza – as in Ian Stasinowski of Norwood's 1978 premiership side. Something about him throwing a family-sized pizza box on the fire in the lounge bar and setting the chimney alight.

He blamed 'Robert of Adelaide' Bond. Bondy had decamped the scene in a taxi as soon as the police arrived – highly suspicious, admittedly – and Stazza might have got away with it except for the 'It wasn't me, Ump' look of mock innocence on his face. Fullbacks are always guilty, of everything.

The regulars were sitting in their usual spots drinking and watching the footy on TV as if having half a dozen fireys in the bar, a couple of cops and a roomful of smoke was nothing out of the ordinary.

The Butcher, who claims to be suffering from a flu-like virus that makes his boots go wobbly, pointed across the street to where his wife Julie was standing on the butcher shop balcony.

'Jules has got little Kate's potty ready in case of stray sparks,' said The Butcher. He seemed reluctant to cross the road with Julie so well armed and launched into another chorus of 'Throw another log on the fire'. Kerry, The Big Fella's sister and The Duke's co-owner, cracked up in hysterical laughter.

The Big Fella, who is still recovering after driving a motorbike kickstart bolt through his leg, was upstairs in the living quarters watching the footy and said he could not be bothered moving, no matter what.

Wendy, just out of hospital herself, kept serving drinks from behind the bar in a courageous display of the *Titanic* spirit, while The Big Fella's wife, Glenys, who is overdue for a holiday, wearily said she was booking into a motel for the night. 'With a spa.'

Then The Doc, who had been playing the pokies in the other bar, appeared in the lounge and asked: 'What's going on?' Followed by: 'Who drank my beer?'; 'Who's winning the footy?'; 'Where's Bond?'; and 'What's the gutter press doing here?'

Meantime, in the dining room next door, the fifty or so men of the Christian Fellowship had their heads bowed in prayer. Were they praying for rescue or were they, like The Doc, unaware of what was happening? God alone knows.

The Monsignor was supposed to have blessed The Duke the previous weekend, so how come, pray tell, the place nearly burned down around us?

Hellfire and damnation, it is enough to drive a man to drink.

9 July 1997

Ducking in and out no way to lunch

CALL ME DULL and boring if you like but I am one of those people who, having gone to lunch, likes to stay there – in the one place if possible.

The idea of going to lunch with the intention of having duck cooked five different ways at five different restaurants in the company of ten middle-aged men strikes me as pure madness, as it is.

Three whole days have passed since the inaugural Duck Walk but give me a Chinese Burn right at this moment and duck fat would drip from my arm.

I cannot recollect who first came up with the idea. Cheong Liew and Philip White did the reconnaissance work to make sure the ducks were ready to serve as soon as we walked into each restaurant, so I hold them responsible, or irresponsible, as the case may be.

Cheong, master chef at the Hilton, gave a running commentary on the food as we were eating it, and Philip, wine writer for the *Tiser*, had the job of wheeling up and down Gouger Street with a trolley suitcase full of pinot noir.

The rest of us comprised a dubious mix of ne'er-do-goods including wine makers and merchants, a publican, a food writer and The Great Lord John 'Rifle' Twining, a man of mysterious ways and means.

The point of the exercise, to the extent that it might laughingly be described as exercise, was to sample duck prepared as the best of its kind by five Asian restaurants. All well and good except duck is a fairly fatty meat and since my disembowelling, it is something I might eat once a month, if that, not five times in the same day, for goodness sake.

For the first two restaurants we stuck to a strict timetable of half-an-hour each and by the third restaurant, Lord Twining had already fallen behind, insisting on draining the pinot left unfinished in the rest of our glasses for the purpose of cross-referencing his tasting notes.

If a flock of geese is a gaggle, someone asked, what do you call a flock of ducks? One suggestion was a draggle and Lord Twining, who had managed to catch us up, thought it might be a giggle, which fairly described what he was like by then.

Our group was beginning to appear a bit bedraggled itself and at one stage Whitey temporarily forgot the combination of the suitcase lock. Lord Twining blanched.

I used to like duck; now if I never see another one it will be too soon. But for the record, here are the restaurants and the dishes, with some of Cheong's remarks in brackets:

Hong Fat – Mandolin Duck (noted for crispness of skin, like eating suckling pig); Ming's – Peking Duck (less greasy than traditional method; original version marbled with fat which squirts hot oil when eaten – Australians could eat no more than two slices of traditional Peking Duck); T-Chow – T-Chow Duck (mellow, gentle flavour, slightly plummy. Recipe unknown as owners will not part with it); Mandarin House – Tea-smoked Duck (marinate it, smoke it in black tea, steam it to dilute the harshness of smoked flavour, deep fry; very tender, not so oily; eat in lotus bun with hoi sin); Grange at Hilton – Cheong's Duck (like Ming's except duck marinated with sorghum grass wine, spring onions, mandarin peel, garlic and ginger; cooked on the pink side).

30 July 1997

Filtering out the nicotine nasties

MY BODY HAS BEEN behaving oddly since I had my last cigarette, detoxing itself with a runny nose, bed spins, clammy flesh, hot flushes, insomnia, rasping chest and frequent pees.

A kinesiologist who I met at a drinks party said the symptoms were perfectly normal. Thank goodness. I thought I was dying.

It needs to be said that, weak as water, I have twice given up smoking, once for eighteen months and the second time for three years, so I suppose there is a fair chance of a third relapse. Even so, mathematical extrapolation gives me six smoke-free years this time around.

The nicotine withdrawal has been not too bad, considering. My mind has been uncommonly alert although this may have more to do with steering well clear of the pub until the automatic association of a drink in one hand and a smoke in the other has subsided.

I haven't much felt like drinking, as it happens, which is an unintended side effect and a definite worry. After a few days, I felt my metabolism had adjusted enough. I took a Codral and went to test drink my resolve and woke up next morning feeling a bit seedy but wonderfully smoke-free and righteous.

It took a week to get over the worst of the withdrawal – not much more than a light flu, as a matter of fact – and it irks me to think that I need never have smoked at all and have needlessly paid all those extra tobacco taxes.

Another regret is that I was never able to master the art of blowing smoke rings which, so far as I can recall, is the reason why I picked up the habit as a teenager in the first place.

Teenagers will continue to smoke in defiance of medical wisdom and the more that governments try to crack down on smoking, the more young people are likely to take it up. In modern movies, the cigarette smokers are the iconoclasts, precisely defined by the tobacco industry and targeted at the youth market.

Besides, teenagers are going to live forever no matter what their poison and I can see their point, up to a point. It is not as if you light up your first cigarette and – poof! – you drop dead, just like that. There is no need to make sure your last will and testament is up to date beforehand or to gather your loved ones around you to say goodbye.

Death from smoking is far more prolonged and painful. I watched my father dying from smoking, as he watched his own father, and I would like to break the cycle, if you do not mind, although it might be a bit late after twenty-something years of addiction.

Now, of course, I can describe myself as a recovering smoker, in much the same way that a recovering alcoholic needs only one drink to tip him or her over the edge.

Having twice failed the test, I can never claim to be a non-smoker. But right now I feel terribly smug at having given up again – another statistic to give the tobacco companies the squits, I hope.

10 September 1997

Fred pulls braised rabbit out of hat

THE CHEF'S SPECIAL chalkboard at The Duke usually offers such hearty fare as corned beef and mustard, mince on toast or lasagne, not 'Braised Rabbit $4.50'.

Rabbit? I could not have been more startled had the chalkboard offered pheasant under glass, ostrega caviar or suckling pig. I thought rabbits had been off the menu since the calicivirus decimated their ranks.

The Duke's chef is a woman called Fred, don't ask me why. I have been having a lot of trouble lately remembering people's names, including people I have known for years, so it is reassuring to know someone called Fred. She will not appreciate being caught in the spotlight like this.

While her fish and chips, steaks and schnitzels are first rate, and her eight-ball skills less so, Fred is not noted for performing culinary magic. So how did she manage to pull a rabbit out of the hat?

The Butcher across the road has a decorative window sign with the word 'Rabbits' on it. The sign is an old one, possibly even a heritage item, which The Butcher says he is unwilling to change even though he cannot remember the last time he had a rabbit to sell.

Indeed, to listen to the scientific community, you would think rabbits had become a threatened species fast approaching extinction since the accidental release of the calicivirus in 1995 from an experimental research station on Wardang Island.

A small piece in the paper the other day reported CSIRO scientist Dr Brian Cooke as saying the rabbit calicivirus had wiped out 95 per cent of rabbits in the Flinders Ranges and at Roxby Downs. Another story reported that millions of mulga trees were sprouting across the northern Flinders because there were so few rabbits left to nip them in the bud.

So where did The Duke's rabbits come from? I asked around the bar and the publican Kieren, The Big Fella, claimed he had personally caught them in the Gammon Ranges, and The Butcher said they were his niece Claudia's pet rabbits. I ignored them both, having been sucked in before.

As often happens at The Duke when the Bull Meter goes off the dial, the only way to get close to the truth is to ask Kerry, Kieren's sister. She said the rabbits came from the Southeast.

Where in the Southeast? Very Southeast. Where, precisely? Southeast. In Victoria. Someone Fred knows. Where's Fred? It's her day off.

I have yet to speak to Fred about it but if she has a secret supply of bunnies, I am sure the CSIRO would like to know about it. Does calicivirus not work in Victoria? Is Jeff Kennett breeding a strain of super bunnies in order to corner the rabbit market?

Someone who worked on Wardang Island tells me the calicivirus attacks the rabbit's immune system and because young bunnies have yet to develop such a system, they are resistant to it. Accordingly, as with myxomatosis, the effectiveness of calicivirus will wax and wane from year to year.

Meantime, Fred's braised rabbit was delicious.

22 October 1997

Reg, top bloke, no worries about that

EACH YEAR at about this time, for no other reason than it has now become a tradition, I pick my Most Valuable Person for the year just passed, and this year, for a change and because I was having difficulty deciding for myself, I rounded up the usual suspects at The Duke.

David Black selected Thredbo hero Stewart Diver, John Bradmore nominated the Myanmar democracy leader Aung San Suu Kyi and Nicola behind the bar chose world 500cc motorbike champion Michael Doohan, which only goes to show what a mixed bag they are.

In particular, I was interested in having the opinion of Reg 'Rent-a-Crowd' Ellis because I knew his choice would be thoughtful and kindly. Except Reg is a hard man to track down when he has his dancing shoes on, as he did last week.

Reg leads a hectic life that would exhaust men half his age. When most people are contemplating settling down and getting their retirement organised, Reg is off tracking down the latest jazz party.

He has an exhaustive video collection of great jazz performances that he likes to show friends at home until dawn breaks, a fate I have so far managed to avoid, touch wood. He also sings like Frank Sinatra when in his 'Rent-a-Crowd' mood.

Reg is excellent company, having an attitude towards friendship that demands little and offers much in return. His favourite response to avoid moments of embarrassment or confrontation is: 'Whatever'. In other words, suit yourself.

I have never heard him put anyone down although, God knows, some have drunkenly deserved it. The most you will get from Reg is a flicker of distaste. He is too busy to be bothered. He is unaccountably popular with women. The prospect of seeing Reg in the nude is not one that appeals to me but you never can tell with women.

Yet life sometimes contains more excitement than Reg's body can withstand and, ashen faced, he has to disappear for two or three days to recover.

My favourite Reg story, verified by the man himself, concerns his fiftieth birthday. He and a group of friends decided to have a big night out on the tiles to celebrate and one of them organised to pick Reg up from home at five in the evening and return him there afterwards.

The night was duly had and Reg, having been delivered home, fell asleep in his armchair, still fully clothed. He awoke some hours later, befuddled, and got on the phone wanting to know why, since it was well after five, his ride was late. 'Reg, you've had your bloody party. It's half past five in the morning.'

It occurred to me that Reg might well be my MVP. I checked it out with The Doc, who said: 'Reg Ellis is my man of the year every year.'

That was good enough for me, and when I finally caught up with him, I said: 'Reg, you are my MVP.'

'Good on you, mate – whatever,' Reg said.

3 December 1997

Lymphing along at the deep end

INEXPLICABLY, I have developed a swimming limp that tends to veer me twenty degrees to the right unless I concentrate hard on not heading that way, which is easier said than done when you are going like a threshing machine just to stay afloat.

I was trying to correct the problem the other day when, disorientated from too many tumble turns, I happened to brush my right knuckle ever-so-lightly along the side of the pool in mid-stroke, so slightly in fact that I hardly noticed it at the time, and it bled barely at all.

Yet there it was the next morning, purple and throbbing angrily, and the day after that, the lymph gland under my left arm became infected as well, and now I have a red-raw, blistered, pus-filled eruption the size of a golf ball nestled painfully in my armpit.

The condition is called lymphadenitis, since you ask, and I am on a course of amoxycillin, an antibiotic that is taking its time.

Even as far back as the Winter Olympics – forgotten them already, have you? – I was taking the amoxycillin three times a day and spending each evening painfully squeezing the inflamed area as comic light relief away from the ice dancing.

I have also taken to walking around either with my left arm held at an uncomfortable 45-degree angle, a winged sparrow, or by resting my hand on my hip, which gives me a jaunty, mardi gras air.

Either way, I am sick of it and it has made me think how life hangs by a very thin thread indeed, and even the superficially most trivial of accidents can become life threatening.

It reminds me of the composer Jean-Baptiste Lully, whose self-inflicted death, while not in quite the same league as Michael Hutchence's or Kurt Cobain's, nevertheless put paid to his musical career just as surely.

JB's demise came as a direct result of conducting a performance of his *Te Deum* before Louis XIV of France in 1687.

The *Te Deum* must contain some highly arousing bits because Jean-Baptiste, beating the time by tapping the floor with his cane, managed to drive the thing through his foot. He subsequently died from gangrene.

I once drove a paper spike through the palm of my left hand and then, a couple of months later, did it again through exactly the same spot. I survived after a tetanus shot and several stiff drinks.

On the radio recently there was a story about how we are taking far too many antibiotics for our own good, and stuffing up our immune system. Try telling that to Monsieur Lully.

I'll stick to the amoxycillin, thank you, and take my chances.

4 March 1998

C'mon, Kieran, light my fire

WE WERE SITTING in The Duke, as one does, engaged in the annual debate about whether it was cold enough yet for Kieran to light the fire in the bar. As usual, I was keen to put my money on Anzac Day.

That was until Kieran was overheard to swear he would not light it on Anzac Day on principle, even though he bloody well knows it rains cats and dogs during The March eight years out of seven and blows a gale.

Last year, though, The March had a beautiful day and the weather stayed mild through to Mother's Day – which Kieran reckoned saved him five tonne of mallee roots.

It is obviously ridiculous to run a book on fire dates when the publican has spiked the result, so JB suggested instead we play a game where you take the name of your first pet and link it to the street name where you first lived.

In my case the result, I said, was 'Joe Panorama' and everyone agreed the name had a certain swashbuckling charm, which gave me a warm inner glow until I realised it actually should have been 'Joe MacKillop'. I kept my mouth shut rather than spoil the moment, of which there are precious few.

Also impressive was Louis's 'Olympia Halifax', as was JB's 'Tiddles Cave'. Doc had 'Tuppence Maxwell', Wayne had 'Spot Wellington', Nicola had 'Nicolo Falmouth', Glenys had 'Smokey Kent' and Kevin had 'Lucky Railway Terrace'.

As you can imagine, we could have continued like this all evening except someone went and asked JB if there were any point to it all. Not that I know of, JB said.

We sat there snacking on JB's cashews and played scissors and paper until I had to retire hurt with bloodied knuckles. Bob turned up in a T-shirt with the muddy imprint of a soccer ball on it, which I told him looked like the DNA of a goalie.

Kerry then told an odd story about how Misha had brought a Smokemart bag full of crabs into the front bar, which she had refused to put in the fridge because they stunk, so he left them on a back table.

The crabs disappeared when Ron did and Misha, having wrongly accused someone else, used a pool cue to lay waste to a twenty-first birthday gathering around the juke box. Meantime, Ron was in his garage already tucking into the crabs with lashings of vinegar. Beautiful, was all he had to say when Kerry rang to tell him about the fracas.

Outside, it was sprinkling rain. The West Coast farmers who were here for the Adelaide test match had forecast we would have a wet winter because a wood pigeon had nested twice over the summer in the vine under the verandah.

The West Coasters sow their crops on the first of May, come hell or high water, and Kieran reckoned they would be pleased with the rain. By now, it was bucketing down outside, and cold inside.

All this happened on Monday. I wasn't there but at Tuesday lunchtime Kieran, blue-lipped and his arthritic leg giving him hell, finally relented and lit the fire.

22 April 1998

Minor footnote in athletic history

MY MAIN CLAIM to fame is I can wiggle my ears. Truly. Very few other people can wiggle their ears, it seems, and I once won ten dollars doing it as a party trick.

Curiously, though, I cannot wiggle them while smiling. So I have yet to see myself do it because every time I try to watch what happens in the mirror, it cracks me up.

Other people can turn their eyes in, or make their noses twitch, or curl their tongues. Yet others have talents of a more athletic bent: vaulter Emma George and her pole; cyclist Stuart O'Grady and his pushbike; runner Cathy Freeman and her flag; swimmer Michael Klim's haircut.

The point is we all have special gifts, a little something that sets us apart from almost everyone else. Lance Campbell's forte is the standing long jump. He stands with his feet together and then bounds forward, like a long jump without the run-up.

He did it in The Duke two nights ago by leaping – without a warm-up or even a stretch – the width of the tiled hearth, a distance of roughly two metres, which is far, far longer than Lance is tall. He was sober at the time, in case you were wondering.

Amid much back-slapping, Lance shrugged it off as nothing special, explaining that in his prime he had leapt three metres (9'8"), which he thought might have been enough to win him the gold medal in any of the four Olympic Games held between 1900 and 1912, when the standing long jump was an actual event. I couldn't even fall down the stairs that far.

Lance put it down to being double jointed and said as a younger man he could scratch behind his left ear with his right toe, and could still eat lunch off the soles of his feet.

So, perched atop a bar stool, Lance pulled both his feet inwards and upwards until the soles were positioned together upside down.

Enjoying himself by now, he related how he once toured the UK as a dogsbody with a theatre company. Actors being especially superstitious souls, every time they entered a new theatre they made Lance leap up from the stalls onto the stage for good luck.

Until, at Whitehaven, in The Lakes District, he cracked both his shins and instead of taking it in his stride, two weeks later, at Aberystwyth in Wales, he failed to jump a babbling brook and took a chunk out of his right shin.

Septicemia set in and he would have lost his leg had not the antibiotics worked.

It was Lance's night. Later, in his capacity as head of the local residents' group, he addressed a pub gathering on traffic problems and some powerbrokers are now wondering if he can be drafted for the next council election: Vote 1 The Human Frog.

Afterwards, some sad news, I am afraid. Lance checked the Net and found that American athlete Ray Ewry won the standing long jump in those early Olympics and set the world record of 3.47 metres (11'3") which lasted until the event was finally discarded in 1938. Lance says he will settle for the silver.

10 June 1998

The ghost who walks

BACK HOME FROM West Terrace Cemetery, shivering and covered in slime from here to suppertime – the next time I express a desire to take a walk along a different route, do sit on me, someone.

The idea was simple enough – to walk all the way around the cemetery perimeter. Instead of which I was sucked up to my knees in the wetlands and had to use both hands to lift each leg from the ooze, and toppled over several times into the quagmire.

At this time of the year, the parklands north of the cemetery, off the beaten track, are particularly wet and the army should be using the area for survival exercises. A whole battalion could be hidden in any of the gullies.

After twenty minutes, bedraggled and exhausted, I abandoned the walk as a sick joke and decided to cut back through the cemetery. It was dark and thundery.

That was all I needed, another soaking and another dose of the flu, as if one hit already this winter was insufficient punishment. At least four types of flu were doing the rounds, according to the Health Commission. Beyond caring and trudging through the graveyard, I wondered how many other flu victims had their resting places hereabouts.

We simply do not put enough detail on our headstones nowadays. From the early headstones it was possible to ascertain the occupant's name, age, birthplace, marital status, method and location of death, and even a social commentary on the times: 'Taken In The 1998 Flu Epidemic'.

Now we are lucky to get much more than a name, age and an unimaginative final message such as: 'In God's Care'. If only.

One of my favourite headstones is the pink stone one in the shape of a full-scale bass drum. On it is written: 'Leonard Massey. Late Drummer. John Martin's Orchestra. Accidentally Killed Dec 28, 1939'. I cannot help wondering if the big drum played a part in poor Leonard's demise.

How we regard the trappings of death reveals a lot about a society's mental health, if you ask me, and our current attitude seems to be to ignore it and it might go away.

But it never does. Life snaps, you die.

By now the lactic acid from the exertions in the mud had kicked me in the calves, reducing my steps to a shuffle, and in a sombre mood I emerged wraith-like in the rain, soaked, smeared in mud and with bullrushes clinging Velcro-like to my clothes. I can only guess what it looked like to the elderly woman coming towards me on the cemetery path.

'Mornin',' I said, as we passed. She ignored me, as you should when confronted by a muddy graveyard ghost.

8 July 1998

Indebted to you, Nick

TRUE STORY.

A certain Adelaide Hills pub offered a free dinner for two as first prize in a fundraising raffle by the local footy club. The winning couple arrived to find they were the only ones in the dining room and, such was the weather, they took it upon themselves to light the fire in the dining room. Afterwards, they was presented with a bill for eight dollars, marked 'wood fee'.

The publican concerned was not Nick Binns although it could have been, as befits a man who proudly wears a T-shirt emblazoned: 'I'm Nick Binns – Give me all your money!'

Nick is the publican at The Exeter, one of the city's last remaining 'character' pubs, which has no airs or graces – a lot like Nick himself, actually. Some people think he is as tight as a fish's sphincter, which undervalues the watertight qualities of fish.

There is the account of the drinker who put twenty cents in the peanut machine on the Exeter's bar wall, twisted the handle and had just three nuts drop into his waiting palm. 'What do you call this?' he said, holding out his hand. Nick: 'Profit.'

Wine writer Philip White, an Exeter regular, remembers the time when he wandered into the front bar and said: 'Nick, I should very much enjoy a cleansing ale, but I am a bit short of cash at the moment. I wonder if you would mind covering me, old friend?' Nick: 'What, at these prices!'

It is said Nick never ventures out in public with more than ten dollars in his pocket in case he is mugged. Or how about this: Nick was in the front bar, early one Sunday morning, counting the takings from the previous night, when suddenly a searing pain ripped across his chest. Fearing a heart attack, he rang for an ambulance.

When the ambos arrived, Nick was groaning in agony, clutching his chest with one hand and continuing to count his money with the other. He made the ambos wait until he had finished.

I do not drink at The Ex as often as I once did but happened to be passing the other day and popped in for a chat. Nick greeted me with: 'You owe me fifty dollars!' He said I had not coughed up the petrol money from having stayed with a group of petanque friends on his River Murray houseboat last April – yes, April.

I told him I thought it was a bit rich, having already paid $100 a person for the boat hire, and had assumed the fuel was included in the cost, not a hidden extra.

Wrong, Nick said, although on second thoughts he conceded that because I had not travelled up there with the others on the hire bus but had gone alone, I could make it thirty bucks just for the houseboat fuel.

I handed over the cash and bought Nick a beer, out of grudging admiration, more than anything else, for a legend.

He will probably sue me for suggesting it but I have a sneaking suspicion he really is a generous man deep down, who secretly gives alms to the poor and tends the wounds of lepers in his spare time.

Or perhaps not. The Binns motto is *Nil debit fugit*. Never let a debt go by.

9 September 1998

The light shineth in darkness

HALFWAY ALONG Sturt Street in the city sits Whitmore Square, surrounded by St Vinnie's night shelter, St Lukes Mission, the Salvos hostel, The Gothic Hotel and the back street brothels, which do a brisk trade. At the far end of Sturt Street, West Terrace Cemetery completes the picture.

If I stand on tip-toes in my bedroom, in the manner intended by Sydney real estate agents when they mention 'harbour views', I can just see the tops of the Moreton Bay fig trees on Whitmore Square.

I am always using the Square as a walkway to get to and from the Central Market, ditto for the restaurants in Gouger Street and sometimes to appear in the courts on Victoria Square to defend myself in these increasingly litigious and punishing times. On an early spring morn, it is simply glorious.

Late afternoon, before Vinnie's opens, is not the best time to be passing through the Square, however: the drunks are drunk by then and often abusive; the addicts, on the lookout for a night fix, assess your potential as a hold-up victim; and the bewildered simply swear at you and urinate on their plastic sandals.

Set in the lush grass is a giant chess board made from slabs of black and white concrete, presumably intended for the purpose of playing human chess. It would be no problem finding thirty-two people lying hereabouts to be the chess pieces although how you are supposed to be a bishop when you can barely scratch yourself is beyond me.

I tend to steer clear of the public toilet at the Wright Street end of the Square because my mother warned me about such places. It should not be closed, however; there would be a sudden rise in the incidence of indecent exposure, which is the last thing the neighbourhood needs.

Paradoxically, the Square seems to be safer at night when the shelters are full. One young woman I know goes on late walkabouts through the Square carrying a tumbler of whisky for company. 'Putting Beirut to bed,' she calls it, and she has never been set upon.

Now, lo and behold, a letter has turned up from the City of Adelaide outlining plans to put new lights along the two pathways running north-south/east-west through the Square. The paths cross to form a crucifix, which should look very impressive all lit-up at Easter.

The problem, though, is I never use those paths but instead take the diagonal one which runs from Sturt Street, on the western side, to Wright Street, on the north-east corner. It is the shortest route to where I want to go and people always take shortcuts, no matter which direction the Civic Mind wishes them to travel. The same Civic Mind that gave us the giant chess board.

Another thing: The local Neighbourhood Watch newsletter, which used to contain a long list of local murders, rapes, assaults, break-ins and so on, suddenly dropped the statistics about six months ago. All it tells us now is how to obtain engraving pens, to lock up after yourself and where to get a good pub meal.

Stick your head in the sand and who can see the light?

28 October 1998

Weight for age bad health bet

DURING THE Spring Racing Carnival there were moments of near obscenity at The Duke when the lounge resembled the bar scene from *Star Wars*, leaving no doubt whatever in my mind that alcohol shrinks the brain.

I mean to say, people have lost their shirts at the races before, but to lose them en masse dancing late night jiggedy-jig in the lounge bar is something else again. Even A.G. 'Gilly' Gill, a man normally with a strong constitution, found the scene unnerving.

At one point, a Papal Emissary appeared silently from the night and sat outside under the vine, his chest adorned with a name tag from St Vinnie's shelter with the hand-printed words: 'Does not know own name'.

In the sober aftermath, the worst of it was the nightmarish memory of The Duck and The Bear dancing topless cheek-to-cheek. One really has to wonder where all the advances in medical science are taking us.

The one place where medicine does not much take itself is into pubs, more's the pity. The Duke might have exuded an air of drunken wellness and bonhomie on Cup night, but even a casual observer quickly would have determined that most of us would not pass the muster in a medical examination.

The Publican himself is a walking disaster area; Glenys has a bung knee; Gilly and The Butcher have the gout; Reg needs a replacement hip but keeps putting it off; almost everyone is overweight and has a shocking diet; blood pressure and cholesterol levels are sky high; a bad cold is always doing the rounds; asthma and allergies are common;

alcoholism is endemic, as is emphysema; at least one person a week bears the scars of the latest mugging; and there is a sprinkling of bewildered characters with nowhere else to go.

The sad fact is, we are mostly men, and men are notoriously reluctant to seek medical advice until, having reached the point where the pain is excruciating, they have no choice. No wonder men die earlier than women – although, as The Doc points out, women live longer because they do not have wives.

As an aside, hotel bar staff have to pay higher life insurance premiums even if they don't personally smoke or drink. Just being in the same atmosphere as their customers is sufficient to put them in the high risk category.

Obviously, the Health Commission should be putting resources into getting proper health advice into pubs. It might be something as simple as a Living Health pinboard, offering a selection of information brochures and useful phone numbers. Or a touch screen, even better.

Or how about a wall mounted, do-it-yourself blood pressure unit, for example? Some pubs already have a coin-in-the-slot breathalyser machine and it should be possible to test blood pressure on the same basis.

Perhaps urine tests could be offered as well, although special care would need to be taken with the storage of specimen bottles, well away from the drinks' shelf. Maybe an opening also exists for on-the-spot pregnancy tests.

All I am saying is that based on the unclad, paunchy evidence of Cup night, there was enough raw material on show to justify an outreach health project at The Duke.

18 November 1998

Thunderclouds over the Prairie

SO FAMILIAR is the landscape of the northern Flinders Ranges that when you go there it is like driving through a Heysen painting or, to assist those aged under thirty, a TV commercial for a four-wheel-drive vehicle.

Nothing, however, prepares you for the heat. The water from the cold tap runs hot, the blistering wind whistles through the bullet-holes in the road signs, and petrol is 85 cents a litre at Blinman when it's 61 cents in Adelaide.

It is supposed to be the rainy season there now, the aftermath of tropical depressions and cyclones way up north. The last big downpour worth remembering at Parachilna was in 1989, when it rained for a week. All the creeks flooded; fences and trees were ripped out. The locals do not remember it fondly.

Making my first trip to the Flinders, I had intended to get into the swing by buying a swag and sleeping outdoors. Then I heard the rainy forecast and, anyway, such is the size of a swag I would need a ute in order to carry it around.

So I stayed instead in the air conditioned comfort of the Prairie Hotel, run by Jane Fargher, at Parachilna. When the first storms were forecast on New Year's Eve, I was ready for it, a cold beer in hand and a weather eye cocked towards the cloudless, copper sulphate sunset. No rain seemed imminent.

On New Year's Day, thunderheads began to build tantalisingly from noon onwards, but, having taken a glance down at Parachilna, the clouds split in two, one half going over the ranges in the east and the other half across the dry saltbed of Lake Torrens to the west.

Later in the evening, the local stockmen and rousabouts were surfacing from their New Year's Eve revelry, eyes bloodshot and puffy, and swearing off Bundy forever. Lou ordered an iced coffee and dropped his loose change on the wooden floor. 'Away, you bastards!' he snarled, as a warning to the rest of bar.

Brothers David and Peter, from Commodore Station down the road, who were last seen heading off on New Year's Eve each armed with a bottle of Bundy, seemed unaffected by the weather, having spent the worst of the day's heat sleeping it off. Outside, Dave's kelpie vomited what looked like Bundy and Coke in the darkness. Mazz said the rain would not necessarily make it cooler, just muggier, and Mim said even a pool of ankle-deep water was enough to keep her cool.

The next evening, 2 January, after watching the clouds gather all afternoon over the ranges, news finally came through that it was raining at Blinman, 32 kilometres away, but the cloud cover had knocked out the satellite TV. Typical, said the Prairie's chef Bart. When it actually rains and you want to be inside watching TV, you can't.

Ross Fargher popped in from the family homestead up the road and said it had been 44 degrees yesterday on the verandah but felt hotter today. Everyone agreed, and upwardly revised their temperature guesstimates in a spread from 44 to 48 degrees.

The rain never made it to Parachilna in the week I was there. I told Jane I'd send her a thermometer to end the arguments but she said not to bother, it would spoil the fun.

13 January 1999

Warrawong on the right track

THE DINING MUSIC at Warrawong Sanctuary, in the Adelaide Hills, comes in waves of electronic tinkling and sighing that is supposed to evoke the various moods of nature and put you in the right frame of mind for a dusk walking tour.

Similar compositions, I believe, are available at Australian Geographic or ABC shops, in the bin marked 'Moody Teenaged Girls'. It put me in a strange mood of my own and odd titles kept popping into my head: 'Dangling dead by a rope in an ice crevasse'; or 'Drowning slowly in a frigid fjord'.

A young man with a flaming red ponytail and his girl-friend, who bit her fingernails, were seated at the next table. Beyond them, through the picture window, dozens of rainbow lorikeets climbed over one another, squabbling to get at the seed trays and bowls of honeywater left for them in the trees outside.

The couple watched the birds flitting around for a while before he finally said to her: 'Do you think they can fly off?' Uh-huh.

It is easy to imagine how, in colonial times, the same couple would have imported cats from Mother England to deal with the potoroos and bettongs that the early settlers mistook for large rats. Entranced by the lorikeets, they did not notice Lesley, the tame potoroo, at their feet under the table.

Our tour group was introduced first to the speckled hens, Warrawong's early warning fox alarms although they do not know it and it is better left unsaid within their earshot. The exclusion of foxes and cats is the secret behind Warrawong's extraordinary breeding success.

Another warning: pat kangaroos as much as you like but not on the head. The sanctuary males, even though they have been desexed, paw each other around the head to determine their rutting rights in the mob.

Touch one on the head and he might lean back on his tail and rip your guts out with his hind legs – or take a particular liking to you. Either way, not a pleasant thought.

Our tour guide next took us to a pond where, he said, long-necked tortoises resided, remarkable for their ability while swimming to breathe from any and every orifice, head down, bum up. An interesting party trick.

I suppose there must be some kind of tactical benefit in being able to breathe through your tail if you are a tortoise although, speaking personally, it is rather an unpleasant thought.

No long-necked tortoise showed itself, nor did a platypus, which disgruntled some members of the tour party. Our guide apologised as if the platypus, not understanding it was there for our amusement, had uselessly failed to perform on cue.

Meantime, somewhere unseen in the pond, a platypus was going about its platypussy business and could not give a tortoise's bum for what we thought, which only added to the moment.

Some things, money still cannot buy. Which is exactly how John Wamsley, the founder and driving force behind Warrawong, seems to like it. Shame about the music, though.

3 March 1999

Tell them where you heard it first

THE WHISPERING WALL, in the Barossa Valley, is one of those places most people visit just twice or maybe thrice in their lifetimes: as a child, a parent and possibly as a grandparent.

Such a pity, really, because it is South Australia's only serious contender as the Eighth Wonder of the World. The proposition behind the Whispering Wall is simple enough: two people stand on the platforms at each end of the curved dam wall, perhaps 100 metres apart, and can converse even at a whisper.

By the way, it would be interesting to know if the curve of the dam wall which produces the desired effect was deliberately designed that way, or was it a case of serendipity? My money is on a fluke.

A visit is best done in pairs; a solitary person could stand there all day and not get the point of it.

It is also a great way to eavesdrop on the conversations of lovey-dovey couples who are seemingly unaware they can be heard by everyone else within earshot. Listening to what one party intends to do to the other party in the privacy of their spa bath that afternoon at four o'clock can be very off-putting indeed. The wall should be given an R-rating.

Yet it seems even the innocent pleasures of the Whispering Wall are about to fall victim to the user-pays principle.

I happened to be at the Whispering Wall last Friday, showing it off to an interstate visitor before we did the rounds of the Barossa wineries, and was surprised to find a yellow sign at the near end of the dam wall: TEMPORARILY OUT OF ORDER.

How odd, I thought, as I sent the visitor to the far end where he stood silently staring at the wall directly in front of his face.

'You have to talk,' I whispered from my end, 'otherwise it doesn't work.'

He waved furiously at me to come across to his side, shouting, 'Come here!' so I could hear him.

Perplexed, I wandered across to see what was up and you can imagine my astonishment at finding a one-dollar coin-in-the-slot unit, about the same size as a domestic gas meter, newly attached to the wall.

It had a volume control knob on it and a series of coloured buttons which offered a selection of foreign languages.

Now, I am all for turning a quick buck where possible, even to the extent of accepting the Coke machine that sits atop Uluru to slake the thirsts of American tourists.

But there are limits and it is particularly depressing to think we have reached such a low financial ebb in this State that a dollar coin is now necessary to make the Whispering Wall talk.

Underneath the unit was a cardboard sign which said it would be switched on this Thursday, 1 April.

30 March 1999

Best memories last forever

TEN YEARS AGO this Queen's Birthday long weekend, my father, Jack, died in Geelong.

He had been unwell for a long time, frequently bedridden, speaking in small, quick breaths, and his fragile, tissue-paper skin glowed in the half light. He was once big and strong. Emphysema takes it out of man.

Towards the end, his blood circulation was constricted to the point where he constantly felt so hot that his bedroom window had to be kept wide open no matter how cold it was outside, and it gets very cold indeed in Geelong. Bedside visitors had to sit in their coats and hats.

I had been there with him at Easter 1989 and the Sunday was a lovely, soft day. Dad was well enough to get out of bed and the two of us sat on the front verandah after Mum went to Mass and we drank a bottle of red label Johnny Walker for medicinal purposes.

I had brought him an expensive bottle of Islay single malt for a change, from which he took one small nip and left it there untouched on the shelf.

I made a mental note to grab the Islay as I left, promising next time to bring him a book instead. All the books I had given him always had my own name written inside the cover to make sure, as I frankly told him, that I got them back after he shuffled off.

We spent the morning reminiscing. I had never heard him open up as much in one sitting, recalling odd snippets of his life such as a dubious tale about how, by flashing his international driver's licence as if it were a police ID, he once had burst into a brothel in Germany to save a drunken business colleague. Hmmm.

We finished the red label. I badgered him to put some of his memories on paper, to leave something behind for his great grandchildren. He showed no interest in doing so, possibly daunted by the enormous quantity of scotch he would need to keep him up to it. It was too late.

He asked when would I be back. I named the June long weekend and we hugged and that was the last I saw of him. My mother rang on the Queen's Birthday Monday to say Dad had died asking after me.

The thing was, at the time I was lying in St Andrew's Hospital, tubes coming out of every orifice, having been operated on for bowel cancer. Mum already had enough to worry about and I had kept my condition secret from her. Damn it.

I made it to the funeral, where I heard that the doctors were amazed by how long he took to die, so strong was his heart. But I knew he had waited because he expected me to turn up to say goodbye, his willpower holding death at bay, until finally he could wait no longer.

Thinking back a decade later, I hold dear the memory of that last Sunday morning together on the front verandah, just the two of us. It was the best of farewells, father and son. And he gave me all the books back.

I just wish I could have explained why I was not there at the end for you, Dad, tears coming to my eyes now.

9 June 1999

Sexy airs on a G-string

FOR SHEER melodic beauty, it is hard to beat a cello, a swooning instrument suited to sighing Edwardian women having a romantic attack of the vapours.

The cello seems to be the flavour of the moment, thanks in part to a recent ABC TV series starring cellist Yo-Yo Ma – great name – and the film *Hilary and Jackie* about the life and death of Jacqueline du Pré, drowned at the height of her powers in the slack, drooling tide of multiple sclerosis.

I would love to be able to play the cello, or the viola. Gradually and without doing it deliberately, I seem to be at a stage of life where, given the choice between playing the drums for Deep Purple or going to hear the Australian Chamber Orchestra, I would choose the ACO.

This from a man whose previous interest in classical music was limited to Mickey Mouse conducting the buckets and mops in *Fantasia* and Procol Harum's *A Whiter Shade of Pale*.

The ACO had them packed to the rafters at the Adelaide Town Hall last time they were here. Artistic director Richard Tognetti did a solo of Dvorak's violin concerto, not something you can hum along with. I have enough trouble pronouncing Dvorak's name.

Bent kneed, violin tucked under the chin, Tognetti took up a stance like a tennis player favouring one leg, poised on the balls of his feet and ready to pounce all over the second serve. Women shifted in their seats.

Tognetti is thought to be rather sexy in some female circles and I suppose he does have a raffish charm, with his straggly blond hair and undernourished appearance. In a certain light he resembles the 100-metre sprinter Matt Shirvington; take a closer look next time.

In fact, all the ACO members are strikingly good looking, as if they were selected by a Hollywood casting agency. The ability to play a musical instrument must count for something, too.

They also smile a lot, taking pleasure in each other's playing, picking up nuances that pass me by altogether. One of the viola players, whom I have identified from the program notes as David Wicks, always looks highly amused. Perhaps he secretly farts.

Good for you, David – such a pleasant change from the grim-faced, old hacks elsewhere who turn up to play as a job of work, looking like they would rather be somewhere else and spoiling it for everyone watching.

Also, the instruments are always ranked according to the age of the players, starting with violins in the hands of the youngsters. The slightly older ones get the violas, onto the cellos, until finally the big grown ups get the basses. Not everyone notices this the first time.

None of this means my musical tastes are more refined, just more appreciative. Some of the modern orchestral stuff still leaves me cold – such as Berio's *Chemins IVb* where, so long as the players started together and finished together, no one seemed to mind what they got up to in between. I thought David was going to wet himself.

There, that's your dollop of culture for the year.

16 June 1999

Yeee-ha! Ride 'em Bronco

THE RED Malvern Star Bronco SX that I picked up from a secondhand furniture shop at the Port for $150 – with a battered red helmet thrown in as well – has fifteen gears of which I have used no more than four: 12, 13, 14 and 15.

I cannot imagine when first gear might come into play. My son tells me it is for riding up a near-vertical, snow-covered mountain, which Adelaide sorely lacks.

My son also says the tyres, although like tractor treads compared to the thin ones I used to have on my school bike, are still not nobbly enough for going around wet corners safely at 40 km/h. Do spare me.

I have never reached 40 km/h even going as hard as I can in top gear downhill in a straight line. Even then, young men on superbikes cruise by me, their legs pedalling at about a third the rate of mine.

In any event, I do not like going too fast because the Bronco SX's brakes are not crash hot – an apt term – and you never know when a moron driving a car is going to do something unexpected.

Like the woman in the black BMW parked on Unley Road who flung the door open right in front of me.

Having no time to brake, I momentarily considered just crashing and executing a double somersault over the door to land perfectly on both feet. Instead I cut blindly into the following traffic, which honked, blasted and abused me.

I began to worry that bike helmets are nowhere near as protective as they appear. They will not prevent your face from being smashed in by an angry truck driver.

While I counted myself lucky to have escaped in one piece – grrr – the woman, though shocked by my language, did not even say she was sorry and merely walked away. I know your numberplate, lady.

Go into any bike shop and the conversation quickly turns to tales of major 'moments' and to comparisons of scrapes, scabs and scars, and to suggested ways of making the streets safer for me and my Bronco SX.

For a start, there are not enough bike lanes and the ones that do exist either do not link up with each other or suddenly run out at the most inappropriate places, such as across the bridge on Morphett Street or near the Thebarton police centre.

A bike lane along a main road is also likely to be a bumpy obstacle course of potholes and manhole covers, littered with a slippery scree of stones and shattered glass.

If I had my way, as a condition for being licensed to drive a car, every damn motorist ought to be made to ride a pushbike for a week once a year.

They would quickly become aware of how vulnerable a cyclist feels in traffic and it would have to make them better drivers – and it would definitely stop them running red lights.

25 August 1999

Tunnel balling hall of fame

NOT EVERYONE, given the opportunity of being immortalised as the first possession getter at Football Park, allows the ball to roll through his legs and has his opponent pick it up and goal.

Allow me to introduce Philip David Ashmead, otherwise known as Clanger, one of a pack of old footballers who frequent The Duke, among them Bear, Stazza, Rocket, Ansett and The Weed.

Clanger Ashmead was once a rover with Central Districts and one of his many claims to fame was to play against North Adelaide in the first game at Footy Park in 1974.

Such a memorable occasion, and the ball went straight to Clanger from the first centre bounce – and, well, a football being the shape it is, it somehow tumbled between his legs. He denies it was a fumble as at no time did he get a hand to the ball.

Perhaps it was nerves. Perhaps it was poor technique. Clanger thinks he may have overtrained. Whatever, his opponent, Tommy Zorick, scooped up the ball, goaled, and his name went into the record books, not Clanger's.

Even though I went plenty of times to Elizabeth Oval in the seventies to watch Ceeentraaaals – only a Geelong supporter could move to Adelaide and randomly pick the Doggies as his local side – I cannot honestly say Clanger stands out in my memory.

To hear him tell it, though, you would have thought his flashy brilliance and immense courage were impossible to miss. As well as his mouth.

Clanger tells the story of Billy Barrott from West Torrens who, during a game at Thebarton in 1973, was lining up the goals from one wing alongside the centre circle, an impossible distance. Clanger kept mouthing off at him. 'Ha-ha! You big girl! Ha-ha! In your dreams!' – or words to that effect.

Billy hoofed it into the trees behind the goals. There is contemporary television footage from which it is estimated the kick went 92 metres and some eyewitnesses said it would have gone clear into Ashley Street had it not been for the trees. Clanger and his big mouth.

Clanger says he was not such a bad kick himself – rovers always exaggerate their kicking prowess – and he tells the story of how in 1976 against Port Adelaide, he took a mark at least 70 metres out from goal at the northern end of Elizabeth Oval.

A howling gale was behind him and, fancying his chances, he slowly went back to line up the kick, even taking the time to pull up his socks. At which point the despairing coach, Gary Window, screamed at the runner to get out there and tell bloody Ashmead to stop mucking about and move the ball on quickly.

Clanger listened to the instructions, waved the runner to stand back, and let fly with an absolute boomer that sailed through the centre of the goal posts a third of the way up. Then he turned to the stunned runner and said: 'Tell the coach not to interfere while I am lining up for goal.'

Never mind the tunnel ball, Clanger has been dying to get that story into print.

1 September 1999

Och aye, pass the taramasalata

In Greek mythology, Icarus was flying to Crete one day when he flew too close to the sun, which melted the wax fittings on his wings, and he fell into the Aegean Sea near where the island of Ikaria now sits.

I sometimes wonder if Irene, the woman I have adopted as my Greek mother, has had a touch too much of the sun as well.

Irene is from Ikaria, a heritage she shares proudly with many of Adelaide's Greek community. Some readers might remember she once ran a great restaurant at West Lakes called Irini's; she also wrote an award-winning cookbook of her own recipes; and now she helps her daughter Tina at the Kitchen Hand shop in Unley.

Irene is a wonderful cook and much else besides: a vibrant, colourful, funny chatterer; a loving mother and grandmother to a growing tribe; and, ahem, still sexy after all this time for a woman who professes no interest in it any longer. Her husband George died just a few years ago, sadly.

I love her dearly, and can excuse almost all her craziness except for how she has always maintained, straight-faced, that the Greeks discovered Scotland.

The Greeks have a lot to be proud of – western civilisation, democracy, the Olympic Games and kalamata olives – and Alexander the Great certainly set off around the eastern Mediterranean to Egypt and away towards Asia Minor and India.

But pardon me, I draw the line at Scotland.

The historical records show that Scotland's ancient inhabitants were the Picts, followed by the Scots themselves, who came from Northern Ireland – not Greece – in the fifth century, then the Vikings, for whom chilly Inverness must have seemed like a summer resort, and so on through to the English.

No mention of any Greeks, though, see that Irene?

Yet she insists a bunch of ancient Greeks one day climbed into a boat on a whim, sailed or rowed out the Mediterranean Sea through the Pillars of Hercules, turned hard right and, not bothering with Portugal, France, Holland or England, headed straight for Scotland.

Whatever for? I have been to Scotland – it is cold and clammy – and the idea of settling there instead of, say, warm and balmy Portugal is incomprehensible, especially if you had to row there all the way from Greece.

But, as if it conclusively settles the matter, Irene argues further that 'scotia' is the Greek word for darkness, hence Scotia-land, Dark Land, Scotland. She even claims the bag-pipes were of Greek origin – though not haggis.

All this, she says, was taught to her as historical fact at primary school on Ikaria. So there.

Why am I bothering to enter into a public discussion on such silliness? Because Irene dared me, that's why.

'You won't do it,' she said, 'because, my dear, you are afraid of the truth. You do, and someone will write in and prove what I am saying is true.'

Please do, and my name is Ryanopoulos.

15 September 1999

Steep learning curve of life

MY SON Paul is at an age when he should be in full bloom, physically speaking, and quite capable of riding his bike non-stop all the way up Queen's Park Hill without making a big song and dance about it.

Never mind where it is – any hill will do so long as it is at least a kilometre long and becomes progressively steeper as it goes up until, just below the crest, it is inclined at 45 degrees or more. The road up Montefiore Hill is a doddle by comparison.

Now you are getting a sense of what I am talking about in the awesome challenge of Queen's Park Hill.

Fathers have always set little tests for their sons, a time-honoured tradition. Mind you, it can go horribly awry sometimes. I have known cases where grown men could not stand the thought of their teenage sons doing better than them – at anything. Son starts a university degree, dad does too; son plays footy, dad puts the boot in; son brings home new girlfriend, dad flirts with her. And so on in a grim display of one-upmanship that damages entire families – fathers and sons the worst.

Back to Queen's Park Hill. I happened to mention in passing to Paul that as teenagers, my school mates and I used to cycle up it as a proof of manhood. There was little else to do with our manhoods back then, as I remember it.

Paul was keen to see this monster so I drove him there and we went all the way down and back up again in the car.

It must have struck the intended nerve because the next day we were perched on our bikes atop Queen's Park Hill and Paul was wanting me to hang onto his wallet and bike lock in order to lighten his load. I refused, saying I used to do the climb with a schoolbag on my back.

Grumbling, off he rolled downhill to the start and I positioned myself a third of the way down since I reckoned he would hit the wall thereabouts on the way up. Were his foot to touch the ground, it would happen there first.

To cut a long climb short, by the time Paul reached me his going was so agonisingly slow, so excruciatingly painful, that I was able to walk up close behind him pushing my bike. I could almost smell the fear of impending failure, or something very much like it.

So I was right there when, with one last shuddering, superhuman lunge, he finally crested The Hill and arched exhaustedly over his handle bars, heaving, heaving for more oxygen.

Meantime, I had hopped on my bike for the last few metres and gave him a congratulatory pat on the shoulder as I rolled past, hoping to leave the impression that I had cycled up the final section without raising so much as a sweat. He was unconvinced, I don't know why.

Yes, he did well. All right, very well indeed, and there is nothing quite like knocking off one of the old man's little tests to put a spring in your step – even if your legs are too wobbly to stand up on.

Now that I think back on it, I am not so sure I remember ever riding up it myself.

22 September 1999

Willunga's tango-dancing fairies

I SHOULD HAVE known the night would turn odd when dear Robyn C., who I last saw eight years ago in London, popped up unexpectedly and said she knew we would meet because she had dreamt about me the previous night.

Robyn is that sort of person and such a happy meeting could only occur at Russell's place in Willunga. Both off centre from the universe.

Russell's place has no name or signage except for a chalk-board out the front which simply says PIZZAS. It opens only on Friday nights, a remarkably laidback attitude displayed by the owner Russell Jeavons, a contract chef in his other life.

I have never met the man and he was not there on my first visit, the night I bumped into Robyn.

Someone thought he might be doing a catering job in Broken Hill. Anyhow, his absence was being covered by Remedy – I presume that's how she spells it – whose belly was bulging to the extent that she could not do up the top of her pants.

Remedy said she was pregnant, thank goodness; I have been caught out like this before, making birth remarks only to realise too late that the woman was just fat.

Our group was seated at one end of a giant slab of redgum for a kitchen table, a privileged position amid the bedlam, and we yakked with little Louisa who demonstrated with swooping hands, sprinkling fingers and slicing palms how the chocolate torte was made. Tie the girl's hands behind her back and she would become mute.

Remedy said the baby was due on 8 February; Louisa said she turned 16 next 9 February; and my birthday is February 10. How's that – all Aquarians!

Even more curious, however, was the slow, sensuous tango dance performed in the back shed – known as The Ballroom – by two beautiful teenage girls in white camisoles and petticoats, with fairy wings. Take my word for it.

As a matter of fact, all of Willunga seems to be in the grip of a tango craze. A poster in one shop window offered classes in Tango Argentino, run by an Adrienne Jarvis, 'artist/tango dancer'.

Other shop windows advertised 'butcher/tango dancer', 'newsagent/tango dancer', 'hardware/tango dancer' and so on along the main street. I am exaggerating, of course, but not by much.

After Russell's fairies had finished their tango, for a sudden change of mood, it was announced they would now go outside in the dark to dig out the cellar. As you do.

And sure enough, while one fairy waited up top, the other climbed into a deep hole in the garden, dragged on a pair of rubber boots and began to shovel dirt into a bucket on a rope pulley. I watched them for a while and could only guess at the symbolism of it all since they did not respond to my questions. Fairies do not speak to humans, and quite right, too.

Willunga has turned very strange since the last time I was there. Fairies at the bottom of the garden, indeed.

29 September 1999

Why do they shoot maggies?

Distant memory. The primary school I attended backed onto a cemetery – the cause of many childhood nightmares, I can tell you – and the magpies used to swoop us in the playground from the cover of the tall pine trees along the fence line.

Since I had a shock of curly blond hair as a youngster, the magpies found me quite irresistible. During their nesting season I had to ward them off by holding a stick above my head everywhere I went.

Little kids nowadays are made to wear ice-cream containers upside down on their heads, with big eyes painted on them, to scare away the maggies. Thanks, but I would still prefer a stick.

Stick or no stick, I have had splendid fun recently riding my bike on the Westside bikeway, the bit along Deacon Avenue at Richmond, and being repeatedly swooped by a magpie opposite where Cowley's has its bakery.

This particular maggie only attacks when you are heading towards the city, never when you're going away. I am convinced he has an early warning system in the form of a piping shrike which always races excitedly ahead as I cross Richmond Road.

The other sign of an impending attack is the wood pigeons, starlings, piping shrikes, mynahs, wrens, willy wagtails, even a pair of rosellas, stringing themselves out along the power line to watch the sport.

Head down, pulse thumping, you belt across the open ground as hard as you can go, grateful for the bike helmet and wraparound sunnies. Even the bird spectators hold their breaths.

And in he comes, always from the direction of the sun, tearing towards you like a black and white missile from over the top of Cowley's. You expect to be hit full blast on the left but, with a mid-air twist at the last moment, he cops you on the right side of the helmet and yodels in delight.

If the sun is out, you can watch his shadow on the ground as he does a victory roll and sets himself for another swoop, and another. No matter how many times he hits me, I always have to grin in exhilaration, and I swear the birds on the wire laugh their beaks off, too.

In the latest attack, though, the fourth and fifth swoops were surely over the top. I was almost at South Road by then and well out of his normal range. Nothing quite like playing up to the crowd, is there?

I read the other day where a police officer had fired two shots – and missed – at a swooping magpie over a public reserve in O'Sullivan's Beach. And I thought the police were trained to spray mace first?

Shooting magpies is beyond the pale and I am glad it is October and the swooping season is over.

I held off writing this column until now, when my maggie's hormones are hopefully in better shape, in order not to attract the attentions of some pistol packin', over-zealous lawman who might take a potshot at him.

I love that maggie and look forward to running the gauntlet with him again next year if he is not shot in the meantime.

6 October 1999

Caught pants down, kilt up

TERRIBLE NEWS, I am afraid – it seems Irene, the girl from Ikaria who I call my Greek mother, was correct all along. The Greeks did discover Scotland.

Remember how I scoffed at Irene's claim? Since then, I have been bombarded from all directions by both Greeks and Scots telling me to get my facts straight.

No more! Please. I concede defeat. I was wrong. Satisfied now, Irene?

While one or two people backed my understandably sceptical view – thanks for that – everyone else was over-whelmingly in favour of Irene's version, led by the redoubtable Tom Scotter, who went to the trouble of sending me a history timeline to prove the point.

The issue, it seems, turns on two historical facts, both of which I concede mean the Greeks had a knowledge of the British Isles at least 2000 years ago.

Firstly, in 325 BC, the Greek seafarer and geographer Pytheas referred to the 'Isles of Pretani', the Pretani being the ancient British peoples such as the Scottish Picts.

Secondly, nearly 400 years later in 120 AD, Ptolemy the Greek provided the first known map of the British Isles. Tom Scotter evidently has access to the internet.

I am also obliged to *Reader's Digest* reader John Maroulis – call me 'MacRoulis' – of Banksia Park, who quoted a 1978 edition as saying Pytheas had set sail from Massalia, now the French port of Marseilles.

MacRoulis continues: 'There, Pytheas fitted his 100 ton ship with square rigs, not the row boat that you had in mind, and did travel all the way to Iceland, passing and exploring many British lands including SKOTIA, the land of SKOTOS, meaning darkness.'

Demitrios Theodoridis, of Broadview, wrote me an interesting letter – rather too long for publication, unfortunately – in which he explored the link between myth and history.

Greek mythology, Demitrios wrote, was a 'huge archive of historical, geographical, medical and astronomical bearing'. He also pointed out the word myth was derived from the Greek verb 'mytheome', meaning 'I say, I narrate'.

The parallel here with the Aboriginal Dreaming is obvious. Jesus, too, used parables, as Demitrios noted.

Even without the supporting evidence, Irene was adamant the Greeks had discovered Scotland, as part of her cultural memory. The written record, while handy as backup, was not vital to her knowing the truth of it.

Even so, it made her pause to think and be silent, however fleetingly.

Now that I have shown her the evidence and conceded defeat, she is cockier than ever and is even laying claim to the Greeks having invented haggis! Spare me.

27 October 1999

Christmas spirit in white fur muff

AS ANY LITTLE GIRL can tell you, the two plum jobs in the Christmas Pageant are to ride that pair of excellent prancing horses Nipper and Nimble.

Few are chosen, however. In the old days when John Martin's ran the pageant, it was darkly rumoured you had to be the granddaughter of a Johnnie's director or closely related to very senior management to get a ride. The selection process was never, ever explained.

My dear friend Sarah grew up dreaming the Nipper or Nimble dream, either one, it mattered not. Instead, she spent every pageant as a little girl sitting with her family on the balcony of the Brecknock Hotel, heart aching, watching the floats pass below.

It seemed hopeless and she grew up telling no one of the secret desire she still harboured in her breast.

And lo and behold, a miracle! Way past her fairy princess prime, the call finally came. Would she like to be in this year's Christmas Pageant?

John Martin's was no more, you see. It was now the Credit Unions Christmas Pageant and Sarah had a contact who said one of the smaller credit unions was short of staff on its float. Would she mind helping to make up the numbers?

Would she mind? Ho-ho-ho!

The problem was, she would have to be Boy Number 6, walking alongside Float 63, carrying a lantern. Not quite the coveted ride on Nipper or Nimble but if she felt let down, Sarah did not let it show.

'I was quite happy to be a boy – I just wanted to take part,' she told me, ever the enthusiast. Sarah certainly does not look like a boy and she has had to put up with a lot of unseemly chiacking about having to stuff a footy sock down her lederhosen, and so on.

But when she turned up for the first costume fitting, ho-ho-ho, another miracle! Instead of being Boy Number 6 with the lantern, she was to be Girl Number 10, in the green coat dress with white fur trim, white fur Cossack hat and white fur muff. I hope it snows for her sake.

Early on, when there were still vacancies on Float 63, Sarah asked some of her girlfriends to join her but they pooh-poohed the very idea, apparently too grown up for such nonsense. Bah-humbug!

Fancy that, being too old to recapture the spirit of a little girl at the pageant. Only Sarah recognised a dream coming true when she saw it.

So how do you feel now, Sarah? 'Excited. I have never been in something like this before, except for ballet as a little girl. It will be fun.'

Keep your eyes peeled next Saturday for the all smiling, all waving Girl Number 10 walking alongside Float 63. Let's hope that in her excitement she remembers to go to the toilet beforehand.

Any final thoughts? 'When you write this, just don't make me look like a sad git.'

Absolutely not! Sarah, by the way, is 32.

10 November 1999

Bar the gate, the affluent are here

THE NIGHT WHEN the three Rebels bikies were shot dead, the noise sounded like someone blowing air through pursed lips like a raspberry and then, about five seconds later, two final pop-pops.

No prizes for guessing where that was, I thought to myself, and rolled over in bed to check the clock at 1.56 am.

I lay there waiting for the screech of tyres but the only sound was one short, get-out-of-the-bloody-way siren burst about ten minutes later. I should have ducked out to investigate but I am not yet completely mad.

In another incident the following week, the police laid siege to a house around the corner from my place where someone was supposed to be armed with a crossbow. Ho hum.

It is said locally that our patch of the city is being gentrified. My *Little Oxford* lists gentrification as the 'upgrade of working class urban areas by arrival of more affluent residents' – meaning The Rebels, I presume. Personally, I preferred it as it was.

Certainly, a lot of the old cottages are being done up and some of the warehouses have been converted into loft apartments, a clear sign of gentrification if ever there was one.

Even the woman in the cottage over the back fence has cleared her back yard of all vegetation in preparation for getting in the landscape gardeners to gentrify it.

They cut down several large trees, one of which was an ornamental fejoa that hung over the back fence and shaded my bedroom in the summer. It also dropped invisible, pin-prick needles all over the place which meant you could not lie naked outside. On balance, I was not sorry to see it go.

The one next to the fejoa, however, was last year's nesting tree for a pair of wood pigeons and it was chopped down as well.

Last summer, their nest was just two metres away from my bedroom window and I had a privileged view of the two chicks being hatched, and then kept a daily watch as they first cheep-cheeped to be fed and grew plump. I witnessed their clumsy first efforts at flight and their final escape, wing hinges squeaking.

The same mum and dad pigeons are there again this year. Each morning as I dress and each evening at sunset, they nestle against each other on the fence directly below the empty space where their nest was last summer, cooing confused, forlorn love. The saddest sight in the world.

I was wondering where all these disturbing events were leading when a $606 power bill arrived, not a gift I had counted on this close to Christmas. Naturally I queried it, but ETSA got the better of me by saying its meter reader, until I happened to be home recently, had not been able to gain access to the property all year because the front gate was locked.

What we had here with the $606 bill was the gap between the estimation and the reality, as if I were to blame for keeping my gate locked.

You would, too, when under siege from gentrification.

17 November 1999

FREE EAST

After Timor, what will he do next?

MY FIRST MEMORY of Andy Alcock – 24 years ago exactly this month – is not a flattering one, although it reflects poorly on my judgement rather than on him.

The Indonesian Army invaded East Timor on 7 December 1975. At the time I was working for 5DN. From out of nowhere Andy rang up to say he was representing the Fretilin Freedom Fighters, or East Timor Resistance, or some such, and was offering himself for interview. Andy who?

As we tried to keep on top of the story, Andrew proved himself to be exceptionally well briefed, angry, lucid and available all hours. We interviewed him a lot over the following days and his bearded face also popped up on the TV news, looking a bit like an untidy Che Guevara. Indeed, I seem to recollect he wore a very fetching beret at one stage.

While he proved to be good radio talent, I cynically had him tagged as an opportunistic, rent-a-crowd revolutionary who, having packed away the last of his anti-Vietnam war banners, had snapped up the East Timor horror as another ready-to-wear cause for protest. I was wrong. Sorry, Andy.

Outside of the campaign, even now I know almost nothing about him. Come to think of it, I do not know how he came to be involved with East Timor in the first place. And he does not know I am writing this because I do not know where to contact him.

I vaguely recollect running across him twenty years ago at the old Institute of Teachers – a chalkie, maybe, but just a guess – and a couple of years ago I heard he was working for the Public Service Association. He once mentioned to me he was interested in a job with Amnesty International but nothing came of it, so far as I am aware. And that's about all I know of Andy Alcock, hardly anything.

We are friendly acquaintances rather than friends. He drops into The Duke very occasionally, softly spoken, wearing his 'Free East Timor' and 'Amnesty International' pins and a half smile of uncertainty. He has always assumed I know the same fine detail about East Timor as he does, which I don't, and so our conversations usually have a lopsided feel to them.

The last time we had a beer together in the pub, the Indonesian-backed murder squads were still laying waste to the Timorese capital Dili. I tried to say something reassuring like: 'This is Jakarta's last gasp, Andy, it won't be long now.' To which he replied, knowing people were being massacred as we spoke: 'Yes, but where are the peace-keeping troops?'

Once the troops were finally dispatched amid all the political posturing and back-slapping, I hope Andy allowed himself a wry smile of satisfaction. While just about everyone else in Australia had the stitch with Timor and successive Australian governments were toadying up to the criminal thugs in Jakarta for almost a quarter century, Andy hung in there regardless.

Goodness knows what kept him at it. Human decency, I suggest.

The East Timorese leaders Xanana Gusmao and Jose Ramos Horta deserve their places in the sun, no doubt, but when the history is written of the independence struggle, let Andy Alcock's name be added to the honour roll as well. He is my Most Valuable Person for 1999.

15 December 1999

The day we went to Victor

IN THE EARLY LIGHT, Encounter Bay was the colour of sewing machine oil and just as smooth; the pterodactyl pelicans glided effortlessly on the mild air; a seal flopped and wallowed alongside a line of white buoys; and I would have given anything to be out there in a boat.

Instead of which I was sitting in the Flinders Room at Whaler's Inn, Victor Harbor, lumped together with an assortment of colleagues to plan all our futures when I have enough trouble organising what I am having for tea.

As if locked away in a luxurious prison camp, such gatherings always make me fidgety after a while. I cannot wait to escape and sit yakking in the bar, where all the really productive ideas arise anyhow.

I arrived at Whaler's Inn feeling stiff and sore from a social game of softball the previous weekend. Attempting a smooth slide into first base, I had produced a tumbledown clown roll that jarred my left hip and skinned my knee.

What I needed now was a hard, sweaty tennis game to run out the soreness. As soon as we were released from the Flinders Room, I took off for a game of doubles.

Very quickly I added a cut hand to my list of injuries after chasing an angled ball and running smack-bang into a brick retaining wall. The others then complained that the blood stains on the balls were putting off their serves. Whatever it takes, I say.

I would have stayed out there longer except, stretching for extra oomph on an overhead smash, I tore my grunt muscle and had to retire hurt. The grunt muscle, in case you were wondering, is the one between, say, the fourth and fifth ribs on the left side if you are a right-hander. Shane Warne tore his while bowling earlier in the summer, as you might remember, and had to be rested.

So I adjourned to the balcony overlooking the court and had a couple of sundowners with the slackers up there. Below, to one side, Johnno was swimming laps in the five-metre pool behind a child security fence.

Time passed pleasantly until on the evening breeze, just audible, a quiet statement of fact more than an urgent cry, came the single word 'Help'. We listened and looked around. 'Help' again, this time a bit louder and sounding exasperated. 'Help! Yes, help, down here. Helllp!'

It was Johnno, still inside the pool fence, fiddling with the child-proof lock, a pole with a knob on top of it. Raising the knob unlatches the gate and a child is too short to do it. The device was not intended as an IQ test for adults.

'I can't get out.'

'Lift the knob.'

'I am.'

'Now push it open.'

'I'm pushing'

'You're pushing a fence panel, Johnno. The gate's the next one along.'

'Orrright! Thanks.'

I laughed so hard my grunt muscle nearly killed me.

As you can imagine, Johnno took a fair amount of ribbing over dinner, to which he responded: 'Aw, I've done far stupider things than that,' and I had to leave the room clutching my side in agony.

1 March 2000

Leadership is the art of self-deception

SOMEONE MUST ONCE have thought I had management prospects because years ago I was sent on a leadership training course at Wirrina, along with a dozen of so other executive wannabes.

The usual suspects were there: the one who insisted on answering every damn question first, and later became a recovering workaholic; the one who thought he was a stand-up comic and has since made it to the upper echelons of management; another who discovered a passion for intensive group counselling sessions and incense sticks; one who went home early after bingeing on the first night and who now drives a cab for a living; and me, who cracked my forehead in the swimming pool and bled profusely.

Before we went on the course, everyone had to fill out a long questionnaire in which we rated ourselves on management skills such as communication, logic, adaptability and so on.

Similar questionnaires were also distributed beforehand to some of our work colleagues who secretly had to rate us on the same skills. Then the two sets of ratings were brought together on the course and compared.

Nearly everyone marked themselves higher than their peers – which was precisely what the trainer desired in order to make his point about how deluded people were about their own leadership skills.

On the other hand, if you happened to score yourself lower than your peers it meant you had an inferiority complex and were not cut out for management. Equal ratings simply aroused suspicions of mutual complicity over a beer, which I still maintain was good management.

In any event, it quickly became apparent the most incompetent among us did not realise they were incompetent. Indeed, they had given themselves wildly unrealistic ratings and, in denial, angrily defended themselves and could not comprehend how their peers could mark them so low.

Indeed, they perceived themselves as highly competent managers as well as the life and soul of everyone's party, when in fact they were wastes of space and socially inept. Recognise anyone so far?

Well, now comes confirmation of what the rest of us already know. Two US psychologists have found that the truly incompetent lack the basic skills to evaluate their performance realistically.

Justin Kruger and David Dunning have told Reuters news agency that based on certain skills – such as logical reasoning and having a sense of humour – most people who are inept never realise it even if everyone else does.

Such delusion occurs in intelligent people as well, according to Kruger and Dunning, who found doctors generally overestimated how well they had done in a test of medical diagnoses.

They also found that gun owners thought they knew more than they did about firearm safety, which was hardly surprising in the US.

How do you tell people they are boring pests when they cannot see it themselves? And why do they keep following me around?

29 March 2000

Fond farewell to John Hickey

JOHN HICKEY drank occasionally at The Duke, which is how I knew him, but his eyes were bad and one Sunday afternoon last month he walked between parked cars and into the path of an oncoming vehicle.

A memorial service for him was held at the Salvation Army's Lindsell Lodge, where he lived, and the other venerable ancients sang 'Beyond the sunset for evermore'. The service was already well under way when I arrived and as I sat down, the Salvo chaplain said: 'Now, Bill, would you take up the collection?'

Typical, I thought, as Bill shuffled straight at me holding out a red velvet bag. Except, groan, I had no money on me, nothing except for a wad of yellow credit card receipts stuffed in my wallet.

'Sorry, Bill, no money,' I whispered, trying not to draw attention to myself.

'WHAT! WHAT'S THAT?' old Bill yelled.

Good grief! Thank you very much, God, now please allow the earth to swallow me. Red faced, I held open my wallet to show Bill: 'No money, sorry.'

He shook his head and shuffled to the next row behind. Meantime, Submarine Pete, another of John's mates from The Duke, arrived and took the first available seat.

Bill finally handed the money bag to the chaplain, then went and stood directly in front of Pete, who leaned back and swung his legs around in order to let Bill pass along the row.

'YOU'RE IN MY SEAT!' It had not been one of Bill's best collection days.

Pete quickly moved along.

By now, others from The Duke had arrived, including barmaid Nicola, the one who had given everyone the wrong time for the service. I made a mental note to speak to her later.

'John was a good man,' the chaplain was saying. 'Unfortunately, in his later years, he suffered from poor eyesight and ... it was a sad end for his day to conclude like that.' Quite.

'It is good to see so many of John's friends here today although it seems some of you were given the wrong time' – dagger looks at Nicola. 'For the benefit of the latecomers, what we did earlier was go around the room and invite people to say what they thought of John. Shall we do that again?'

'Very gentle,' a woman called out from the back. 'Very nice, a real gentleman. He was good company, a very sensible man. I held his hand once and it was a real privilege.'

'Yes, thank you, Dorothy,' the chaplain said. 'Anyone else? Perhaps one of John's friends might like to say a few words?'

'Magnanimous,' Peter offered.

'Now that's a good word – I'm not sure I can even spell it,' the chaplain said, and before anyone else had a chance to be a smarty pants he quickly launched into the next hymn, 'God is with us all the time'.

Afterwards, I told the chaplain John would have enjoyed the service. It certainly made my day.

5 April 2000

Heart-stopping sense of timing

THE OTHER DAY I happened to drop into The Duke on the way to lunch and The Publican* asked me if I had heard the news that JB was in hospital after suffering a heart attack.

Such rumours are always flying around The Duke. The Doc is in hospital having his blood tampered with. Reg is having a leg replaced. Hell's Belle has overdosed on her hormone replacement therapy again. Nicola is having a humour bypass.

I eyed The Publican, a noted practical joker but he said a golfing buddy of JB's had given him the news that very morning and his lawyer was now digging out the will. Hmmm.

True, if a heart attack were doing the rounds, then JB was a prime candidate for it. Only the previous week Hell's Belle had spotted him late at night exerting himself over the pool table, all red faced, sweaty and breathless.

A little aside here. I once white-washed JB at pool, whereupon he dropped his strides, as one is required to do. Unfortunately his jocks came down too, and the sight of him standing there at half mast made me put away my cue for some months.

As an asthmatic, JB finally gave up smoking not long ago, quite an achievement for someone in his fifties who used to stand in the bar with a fag in one hand and a Ventilin puffer in the other.

---

*By this time, The Duke of Brunswick Hotel had changed hands. The Publican was now Steve Cimarosti, not the Big Fella, Kieren ...

Unfortunately, since giving up, he has put on a lot of weight. Together with his breathing problems, this gives the impression of a heart attack about to happen.

He also seems to be going through the male menopause. He drives a Series 5 BMW and when I last rang him, he said he was on the golf course.

But it's Monday morning, I said.

So what? he said.

The British Medical Journal recently confirmed that middle-aged men do experience a reduction in testosterone levels – the mid-life crisis – leading to such symptoms as lethargy, depression, hot flushes and loss of libido.

I do not believe JB's libido is a problem, however.

A group of London doctors has even launched an online consultancy for andropausal men – yes, that is the term – recommending testosterone replacement therapy (TRT). It is even claimed to reduce obesity.

Meantime, The Publican had me thinking perhaps something really was awry, so I suggested we ring JB direct on his mobile phone. If he were alive, he would take the call; if he were lying dead on a gurney, someone else would answer it. Either way, we would know.

I had only punched in half the number when have a guess who walked in. JB himself – and looking fairly robust for him – who thought it was a great joke to be considered dead.

Yes, he had indeed been to hospital that morning, but only to collect some new asthma medication, that's all.

Pleased to hear it, JB, now try www.androscreen.com.

26 April 2000

Where angels fear to tread

A COLLEAGUE of mine catches the Outer Harbour train – one of the few commuters left on that particular hellride after years of official neglect – and he still bothers to tick off passengers who put their feet on the seats. Brave man.

He recently chipped a teenage girl about it and copped a mouthful of projectile abuse, to which he responded simply, ahem, why should he get his pants dirty because of her lack of consideration? Quite.

She remained there simmering with her clodhoppers still on the seat, a surly little poopster, and the minutes passed uncomfortably between them. Unexpectedly, she suddenly moved her feet and said, sorry, but she had had an awful day and she then proceeded to pour out her troubles to him.

He listened and now, whenever he comes across her on the train, she smiles at him, a new friend, and she does not put her feet on the seat when he is about.

My mother automatically smiles hello to people at bus stops and in cafes and will sit down uninvited and chat to them. She is the talkative old dear who teenagers dread to find themselves seated alongside on the overnight bus to Melbourne. The thought makes me smile.

By and large here in Adelaide, we try to get on with one another including the strangers we meet. My mother thinks Adelaide people are singularly hospitable.

My first three impressions of Adelaide as a new arrival here last century were the clean, wide streets, the bad drivers and the friendly shop assistants compared to Melbourne. The same elements still apply although the drivers are far worse.

Unlike my mother, I am not known as an especially friendly person even among those people who like me, although I much prefer to get on with people than not.

The other evening I was playing pool at The Duke. A tall young man was playing on the other table next to mine. Occasionally we had to give each other elbow room in the aisle between the two tables.

With his studded ears, nose, eyebrows, tongue and lips, any more studs and he would have looked like a Glomesh handbag. When he sucked on a cigarette I half expected the smoke to exit through the holes.

He also had several tattoos and on his neck was what looked like a spectacular, swirling constellation. 'That's a great tattoo,' I said. To which he replied, tersely: 'It's a birthmark.'

I grimaced and for no reason at all, he smiled and offered his hand – and all I could think was more germs were transferred by shaking hands than from a kiss on the mouth. I settled for a handshake, nonetheless.

Finally, one of the delights of riding the old Bronco SX most mornings is how the other cyclists and walkers nod and smile as we pass each other. Small acknowledgments between strangers really do get your day off to a flying start.

The lesson in all of this, my friends, is that a smile is a sunny, two-way street. Bring that thought along with you into the twenty-first century.

17 May 2000

Skirting around royal protocol

WHEN THE INVITATION arrived to attend a drinks party at Government House to celebrate the Queen's Birthday, I must admit I left the gold embossed card on my desk for a good while to ponder what to do about it.

As a Republican, I was flummoxed about whether to accept – nothing personal to Her Maj, of course – but after a couple of days, I decided, what the hell, why not? If only to see what the enemy is up to.

Now fast forward to the evening in question. Walking along North Terrace after parking the car, I casually mentioned to The Escort that for some reason no entree card for the occasion had arrived, as should have been the case once you RSVPeed.

Never mind, I added lightly, the original invitation in my pocket would no doubt suffice. In fact, without the entree card, I seriously doubted we would get past the front gate but there was no point in putting The Escort in more of a nervous tizz than she was already in.

You can imagine my surprise, then, when the security guards simply waved us through. As we crunched our way up the gravel driveway, however, an even more horrible thought struck me – I could not actually recall RSVPeeing.

Here we were, me in a tux and black tie and her dressed to kill, about to try to gatecrash Government House.

By now we were at the front door and I expected to be turned away, embarrassingly, at any moment. I felt obliged at this stage to whisper to The Escort that there may have been just the teensiest oversight concerning the RSVP. She stiffened and I had to pull her along by the wrist, whimpering.

Yet, remarkably again, we were ushered straight through, our coats were taken, and we found ourselves queuing to be personally welcomed by the Governor Sir Eric Neale and Lady Neale and the other venerable worthies in line.

I began to relax – then noticed the liveried man around the corner who was taking people's entree cards and calling out their names as they were being greeted by Sir Eric. The Escort groaned and wobbled.

Here, finally, crunch time had come and it was too late, with the Governor in arm's reach, to quietly slip away. Oh St Jude, I thought, we're done for here.

I handed over the invitation card to the man in livery, with a whispered, 'Ahem, this is rather embarrassing but …' and the dear chap did not bat an eyelid but announced us loudly as if we were to the manor born.

'So nice to meet you again,' said Sir Eric, shaking hands. Again? Er, I could not say for certain that I had ever met him, not one-to-one anyway, but who was I to argue in the circumstances?

Which was just fine until Deputy Premier Rob Kerin, who was in the same official welcoming line-up, shook hands and said out loud: 'How the hell did you get in here? I thought the security was better than that.'

Thanks, Kero.

21 June 2000

Hercules of the airways

FOR ALL THE inconvenience and grief it caused, the great 1989 airline pilots' strike also provided ordinary travellers with the rare treat of riding in an RAAF Hercules.

The Hercules fleet was drafted into service as a strike breaker by Prime Minister Bob Hawke. I never thought I would see a Labor PM do such a thing but Bob said the pilots' 30 per cent wage claim was outrageous given their already hefty pay packets. Quite.

Bob said it was not as if you needed to be a Rhodes scholar to be a pilot. No indeed. He was a Rhodes scholar and had flown in World War II although, somewhat unkindly, people suggested it was just a Chipmunk trainer.

The Hercules were noisy, freezing and slow, yet hundreds of grateful travellers used them without complaint. Even now, people can still fondly recall the day they flew in a Hercules, not least Julie, the wife of The Publican Steve.

Julie was still a single woman in August 1989, another reason for fond memories. She and a group of girlfriends had saved for a Hawaiian holiday and they simply had to get to Melbourne to make the connection.

Hercules saved the day, along with a courteous little man in a business suit. But let Julie take up the story.

'I was having trouble doing up the seatbelt. It was one of those lap ones and I couldn't for the life of me find the right connections. We were on a long bench against the cabin wall and the man sitting next to me helped put on the belt, which was really nice of him.

'He asked where I was going and we had a lovely chat, really lovely, until we took off and it was too noisy to talk any more. The girls and I had had a couple of farewell champers the night before and, the next thing, I just nodded off. I woke to find myself snuggled against the gentleman's shoulder. The girls said I'd slept like that all the way.'

At which point, The Publican, who happened to be passing, interrupted: 'I've heard this story before. It's true all right. Ask Jules if she snored like she does now, or drooled on his lapel.'

'Steven! And no, don't bother looking at me like that, he didn't take advantage of me, didn't flick my bra strap or nothing. A real gentleman.' Hmmm.

And the identity of this gallant Sir Galahad, virtuous comforter of young women in the clouds? John Winston Howard, yes, our very own Prime Minister.

I checked the files. In August 1989, John Howard had not long been toppled as Opposition Leader by Andrew Peacock, so he would still have been licking his wounds and plotting his revenge. On us all.

'You never can tell with some people, can you?' No, Julie, you can't. 'Did I ever tell you about the time I sat behind Tom Jones at the Festival Centre and asked him for a kiss, and he did?'

Not now, Julie – the picture of you and John Howard is more than enough for the time being.

5 July 2000

Demolition Des ruins Don's day

IT WAS ONE of those mornings when complete strangers ring to abuse you and half the lawyers in town have written letters threatening to sue for defamation.

The newspaper horoscope for Aquarius, while advising me to take advantage of a change in my personal finances, predicted nothing about my having a car accident later that day. Horoscopes are a con.

I should have listened to what my biorhythms were telling me: give the day up as a bad joke, go home to bed and pull the doona over your head. But if I obeyed my inner voice, I would spend half my life in bed.

In any event, by lunchtime I needed some company to console myself and was driving through the city, using the back streets.

Everyone else must have been running around at the same time doing errands and paying bills because I had to sit there for ages waiting for a break in the traffic on Gouger Street. I might just as well have prayed for Divine Intervention to part the Red Sea.

Bit by bit, however, I nosed out until finally the gap seemed just wide enough to cross over, just the one car on my right turning left into the side street I was exiting.

So off I went and – whack! – was immediately collected by a white Commodore coming from my right. Needless to say, I didn't see him; I can only say he was hidden from my line of sight by the car turning left. No excuse.

The front of my car disintegrated – all moulded plastic and tinfoil – but remarkably the engine was still running and I could drive it out of the way, crunching and clattering, onto the footpath on the other side of the road. The Commodore that hit me finished up fifty metres along Gouger Street.

Feeling bad, I approached to see if the driver was okay.

'Des, did you see that!?' he said incredulously. 'Did you see what just happened!?' 'Er, yes I did, Don. I am the other driver.'

Old mates – only in Adelaide.

The police arrived and, since Don and I were standing there chatting amiably, they wanted to know if we were in the same car and where the other driver was.

One of the cops took me aside and said he would have to formally caution me for failing to give way to the right – the least he could do, I would have thought. Sigh. Then the ambos turned up, then the city council clean-up crew and then the tow trucks. The ambos had nothing to do, thank goodness, but, eyeing the damage to my car, kept asking me if I was hurt. Only my pride.

Later the same afternoon, sitting forlornly over a coffee in Gouger Street and watching the rain pelt down, I spotted Don outside dashing from verandah to verandah, trying to keep dry. The coffee tasted bitter.

Afterwards I was told my car was a write-off. Personally, I thought it looked fixable but it is hard to tell what is worth saving or not in our disposable society. Don's car is still at the repairers.

Meantime, I am thinking of hiring myself out as a crash test dummy. Aaarrghh!

9 August 2000

Irini takes out my Y2K MVP

Irini Germanos' first name means 'peace' in Greek but she was early nicknamed 'Fourtouna', meaning 'stormy'. Quite right, too. The woman burns more energy standing still than most people use riding a bike uphill.

I know because I have ridden a bike uphill and also spent a non-stop September in Irini's company on Ikaria, her Greek island home, by turns loving and cursing her. I mean, how do you cope with a woman who took her bathers to Anzac Cove?

Now in her mid-60s, Irini still has a young woman's bouncy step, swinging one arm out wide, the other folded around her bag. Watching her do the national dance at a taverna at Nas, with that girlish sway of the hips … Opa! Ela!

The real privilege, of course, was to be given entree to her family network.

Irini comes from a tradition of island hospitality where a stranger is treated as an honoured guest. 'You must come in and have a drink, you must have a meal, you must stay the night. I have a flat here, you can stay for as long as you like.'

Her conversation would then jump loudly, illogically, all over the place, easily distracted, one topic overlapping another. Irini's brain did not stay still long enough to be able to make sense all the time.

She said she would like her first grandson to be called Icarus, unfazed at the suggestion he would be tagged 'Icky' at school. Someone in the family needs to take her aside for a quiet word.

She claimed she was once shy. When she was fifteen, she said, she had whacked a cheeky young Greek soldier over the head with her bag. He told her she had insulted his uniform and was in big trouble, so she whacked him again and ran off. Shy my eye.

She worried she was developing a compulsive cleaning disorder. Add it to the list. Or, 'I've been modulated by mosquitoes – you know, chopped into little pieces.' 'Mutilated', I expect, but you can never be certain.

Or Irini, mistress of the sweeping statement. 'The Greeks, they are lazy,' meaning the ones who live in Greece, the men in particular. 'Greeks have been cashing in on their ruins for 2000 years.' 'Greeks make the best bread in the world.'

'Try this peach,' she said one day, offering a piece of roadside fruit. It tasted like a nectarine. 'No! You can argue with me about anything but not about food!'

Then she claimed it was an apple/peach, an ancient line of wild Ikarian peach. So why does it have a smooth, shiny skin? Because, she said, she had washed it. In which case, is an Ikarian peach a nectarine covered in road dust? On and on, the argument lasted for days.

In a cafe later, she complained to the owner about the slow service the last time she was there ... two years earlier – and then went on to complain about her coffee and gave strict instructions on how it should be made in future. She'll be baaaack ...

Irini, apart from your driving, it was a joyous time, I love you dearly, and you are rightly my Most Valuable Personality of the year 2000. No argument.

13 December 2000

Junk mail gets even junkier

IN THE LETTERBOX recently was a Church of Scientology leaflet, 'How Toxic Are You?', which suggested the presence of drugs, chemicals and environmental toxins in your body could leave you feeling dull, lifeless and 'wooden'. Agreed.

We all have our problems but succumbing to the temptation of paying \$60.50 (GST inc.) for 'Clear Body Clear Mind' by the dead L. Ron Hubbard, founder of Scientology, is never going to be one of mine.

By the way, how the Church of Scientology ever managed to obtain recognition as a church is beyond me, relying as it does on luring the young, the insecure and the emotionally unstable with promises of mental alertness and spiritual awareness.

Perhaps the Scientologists, in an unexpected outbreak of generosity, might like to provide free copies of 'Clear Body Clear Mind' to the brutally brainless thugs who prowl the city streets where I live, swapping crumpled *Playboy* centrefolds from ten years ago, enthusiastically smashing into parked cars and snapping off sprinkler heads. Toxic is indeed the word for it.

The hot weather tends to draw them out of the drains at night, along with the cockroaches that are so numerous they crunch underfoot. Or was that a discarded syringe?

The other evening, a car parked around the corner had one number plate at the front and a different one in the hand of a heavily tattooed man who was fiddling with the rear plate, which was different again.

Elsewhere in Adelaide, such activity would be regarded as suspicious; hereabouts it passes unnoticed unless it happens to be your own car being tampered with.

Every couple of months, the local Neighbourhood Watch group distributes a newsletter which contains the latest crime statistics by category.

I thought I had saved all of last year's newsletters but can find just the one for August/September. Perhaps the others were stolen.

Never mind, the August/September statistics are sufficient to make the point: 48 assaults, three sexual assaults, three attempted murders, 11 robberies, 52 damaged vehicles, 220 break-ins and so on, amounting to nearly 400 incidents in all.

When I lived in Para Hills, it would take all year to accumulate such an impressive list. But, of course, there are far more drugs in the city and, as some police estimate, at least 60 per cent of property crimes are committed by addicts in order to support their habits.

Next, arriving in the mail, was a Commonwealth Government brochure entitled 'Burglary is everybody's problem', signed by Senator Amanda Vanstone, Minister for Justice and Customs and Christopher Skase.

Senator Vanstone offered all sorts of tips for preventing household burglary, from locking yourself inside to photographing your valuables. Not a mention anywhere of the link between drugs and burglaries, however.

Her fallback position was to suggest that people obtain a dog. Even the Scientologists appreciate the problem is deeper than that.

7 February 2001

Baynes' legacy home delivered

Someone recently found an old photo of me when I was in my late twenties, smiling optimistically, frizzy side tufts of hair like a koala's and wispy strands still draped across the top.

Although it is photographed in black and white, I recognise the suit – light purple, it was, with crimson lining. Goodness knows why I was so happy.

It must have been taken shortly after I had been hired by Roger Baynes Snr, the founder of Messenger Press. Or Old Roger, as he was known, to distinguish him from his son Young Roger, a mate of mine who is still in the print game at Cadillac Press.

Old Roger used to carry around a little black book from which he knew precisely the financial situation of the company at any given point, well before the Messenger accountant could confirm it.

He was never one to spend money on anything that did not contribute directly to the bottom line. For example, his office had cheap kitchen chairs with chrome legs and vinyl seats and backrests. The desk was an old kitchen table, possibly from the same setting.

His own chair was covered in a brown, corded cloth similar to industrial matting. Years later, I inherited the same lumpy chair that wobbled precariously and finally fell to pieces.

And when it rained, water used to trickle down the inside of the editorial department's wall. Since Old Roger's office was overhead, his wall must have trickled, too. Not that he ever mentioned it.

His approach was very much 'you tell me want you want and I will tell you how to get by without it'. And what arose from his 'do without' attitude was a 'can do' culture of excellence among the workforce, as can happen.

People worked hard, sometimes in fairly primitive conditions, and met tough deadlines because they felt a tremendous personal loyalty to Old Roger and did not want to let him down. People here still talk of the Messenger family, which was his doing.

In the recession of the early 1960s, which hit Port Adelaide businesses particularly hard, Old Roger simply refused to pursue the debts of those who could not afford to pay their advertising bills, even though he could ill-afford it himself. In some cases, individual debts were allowed to float for six months or more, and some probably were never collected in full.

The Port never forgot. Messenger reporters who cover Port Adelaide still hear the words, 'I knew Old Roger Baynes ...' and hear again of the man's rough-diamond virtues.

All of this is by way of acknowledging the Messenger group of newspapers turns fifty next Sunday 11 March. Thanks, Roger.

7 March 2001

Adelaide: living in the fast lane

CAMERON KELLEHER is an old mate, going back twenty years or so to when we used to sit at adjoining desks on Friday afternoons, telling ribald jokes to put us in the mood for a beer at the Portland Hotel after work.

Cam had a dry wit. Once a female staff member burst into the newsroom, dark as thunder, shimmering with rage, as if she had popped a psycho pill. Everyone sat back in stunned silence as she clattered back and forth between the rows of desks, swearing and misting the air with her furious spittle.

Cameron waited for a lull and said: 'Okay, Barb, I give up, what's the joke?'

He has since done rather well. He had an illustrious Fleet Street career as a sports journalist and is now the media manager of Jaguar Racing's Formula One Grand Prix team. F1 driver Eddie Irvine is a mate of his and the F1 corporate suits also apparently love his laidback, world-weary 'Aussie bloke' persona.

Last year as a publicity stunt, Cameron somehow got the New York Police Department to allow a Jaguar Racing car with Eddie Irvine at the wheel to tear down Broadway to Times Square. A few words of half-sophisticated strine apparently work wonders even with the NYPD Blue.

He was in town recently and we met for a steak and a bottle of red wine at Gaucho's. Quite a treat, I would have thought, for someone who lives in a land where the beef sausages give you mad cow disease, the sheep are infected with foot and mouth, and a good red wine costs ten times as much as in Gouger Street.

Everything was going fine until I told Cameron, excuse me, would he mind going outside if he wanted to smoke? A lovely moment, three and a half years since my last fag.

He huffed and puffed and spluttered: 'Adelaide is the PC capital of the world!' As in Political Correctness.

He went on to moan about all the other pleasures he was denied here, like driving when drunk, but it was the smoking ban in restaurants that really got up his nose. Stiff.

Later on we caught up with a group of his family and friends at the Brecknock. Among them was china painter Susan 'Gilly' MacGillivray, whom I asked whether she agreed that Adelaide was the PC capital of the world?

'Yes, there do seem to be a lot of them but I would be surprised if Adelaide had more personal computers than anywhere else.'

Cameron groaned. Then his lovely mum and dad, Pat and George, walked into the bar.

'George,' I said, 'what do the initials PC mean to you?'

He thought for a moment and said: 'Police constable.'

Cameron turned to me and said: 'Isn't it time you went?'

Cop you later, Cam.

28 March 2001

Matching lives with cut-outs

BY NOW, many of you will already have nominated your Peoplescape hero and there is something you should know – I am a judge.

Do not be put off. There are other judges, too, headed by the estimable Betty Churcher, former head of the National Gallery in Canberra. I doubt my whole family will make it through the selection process.

As reported in Messenger newspapers, Peoplescape will see 5000 cut-out figures of 'significant' Australians erected in the sloping lawn outside Parliament House, Canberra, next November.

I was in Canberra for the official launch by actor Kevin Harrington, who also played 'Kevin' in the TV series *Seachange*. Kevin had created a cut-out to honour his mate Geoffrey, a bush poet; Betty Churcher had done one of Aboriginal artist Albert Namatjira.

I stood behind the Parliament House Landscape Services crew – they looked just like cut-outs in their matching Akubras and King Gees – wondering how they were going to mow the lawn between the cut-outs. Growth retardant will be heavily used, they assured me.

I am still thinking about who to nominate for Peoplescape though my maternal grandfather John Hughes is a possibility.

After World War I was over – a time beyond memory for most people now – the survivors returned home in dribs and drabs, John among them.

He had been an Assault Pioneer corporal in France where he was gassed, shot and wounded, and won a bravery medal after leading his unit in digging a communications trench under heavy enemy fire. Quite a hero.

John married Annie Shadforth, who was a nurse in France. The official military records suggest two occasions when they were in the same vicinity and their paths might have crossed. I suspect theirs is a remarkable love story.

I remember John – in a nursing home towards the end of his life – as a smelly old fella in flannelette pyjamas. His life had become a drunken shadowland by then, as did the lives of so many other veterans.

Even though I had no idea of his war record at the time, I do remember how his ruddy face used to light up whenever I visited him in my school cadet uniform. His tobacco-stained fingers would gently touch the Rising Sun badge on my slouch hat.

John had a background influence over my life in family ways that grow more significant with the passing years, though the influences are frankly too problematic to name him as a Peoplescape figure.

Annie, who died before I was born but whose life was even more heroic than John's in my mother's opinion, is also a possible candidate. My mother should nominate her.

Feel for me – I only have to help choose 5000 of them, for goodness sake!

4 April 2001

A pilgrimage to Gallipoli

LAST ANZAC DAY, in Melbourne for the dawn service at the Shrine of Remembrance, 'God Save The Queen' was played in almost dead silence despite the best, bull-throated urgings of the Victorian RSL president Bruce Ruxton.

Only when the band struck up our own dirge of a national anthem did people rouse themselves to mumble the half-remembered words, finding full, roaring voice for the refrain 'Advance Australia Fair'. A proud moment.

Five months later, overlooking the gullies and ravines above Anzac Cove itself, the Turkish taxi driver played a tape of 'Waltzing Matilda' and displayed a Digger's bullet which he said had been found on the battlefield.

At one stage in the battle, the driver said, the Turkish troops, outnumbered and fearful of being overrun, appealed to their commander Ataturk to call a retreat.

Instead of which he ordered them to remain in the trenches and fight, saying should they die in battle they surely would enter paradise that very day. Not a bad pep talk, and the rest is history.

Ataturk's command bunker is on top of the highest hill. It takes two hours to walk from there slowly down the ridge line towards Anzac Cove, along the same bitumen road up which the taxi had travelled.

Turkish memorials are located on the left of the road – the high ground – and the Anzac cemeteries are on the lower side where the Diggers fell. Most of the gravestones, although they have names, are marked 'Believed to be buried here'.

Only gradually does it become apparent that the road follows No Man's Land, just a single lane wide, and what look like drainage channels are actually the original trenches, still largely intact. The troops could spit at each other, they were that close.

They mounted repeated bayonet attacks, and the machineguns mowed them down and 12,000 Australians were slaughtered. Every one of them had a life to lead back home.

The main Australian cemetery is at Lone Pine, about two-thirds of the way down. In the chill shadow of the pine trees among the graves, the breeze sighing through the branches, you wonder how they stayed there fighting, day after day for eight bloody months, sometimes going forward, sometimes backward, but going nowhere.

At Anzac Cove, anyone who has been there is struck by the tiny strip of beach – the length of a cricket pitch wide – and the steep cliffs. Such a stupid, stupid place to die.

By first light on 15 April, 1500 Anzacs were dead, many of them having drowned under the weight of their packs after stumbling in the water.

Should Judgement Day be tomorrow and the dead rise again, I should very much like to be on Gallipoli Peninsula to hear what the young men think of what occurred there 86 years ago.

Not much, I expect.

25 April 2001

Submarine Pete feels his age

RAN INTO Submarine Pete the other afternoon at The Duke. He looked out of sorts, the right side of his face a horrible mess of scabs as if he had spent six hours in make-up for a horror movie.

Apparently he had fallen off his bike again.

'Pete,' I nodded, 'how are your problems?' I meant it as a throwaway greeting, not a genuine enquiry.

'Problems ... where do I start?' he sighed, his one good eye looking shell-shocked. Pete is the sort of bloke who would worry about catching tetanus from a guillotine blade.

Last year, his various misadventures were given three mentions in these columns and he told me his New Year's resolution was to score four hits this year. Here is the first and, Pete, the falling off your bike routine is losing its novelty value, let me tell you.

'Coming to my fiftieth?' he asked.

'Nope, when is it?'

'Next month.'

'Won't be here.'

'What, all month?'

'Okay, but I'm not writing anything about it.'

'No probs, just bring a present.'

'How about a gift voucher for plastic surgery?'

Mind you, Steve the Publican was looking not much better. He was sporting a tremendous shiner after failing to duck an incoming chair that had been tossed across the bar by Boof the previous evening, in mysterious circumstances which no one wanted to discuss.

Curious, Your Honour, because I had been drinking with Boof on the night in question and he seemed, yes, high-spirited but, no, not even close to a chair-tossing mood when I left him. Indeed, he had seemed a kinder, warmer person than usual.

Later, a handwritten note appeared on the noticeboard: 'Chair Throwing Event every Wednesday. See Steve for Entry Form'.

Pete, meantime, was complaining about how dark it was in the mornings, yet to realise he had not turned back the clock when daylight saving finished.

Another regular was reminiscing about the time when pure vanilla essence, which had a skyrocket alcohol content, could still be purchased cheaply at supermarkets. Great days.

A losing punter then cursed at the Sky TV, complaining the jockey had made so little effort that the stewards should check him for deep vein thrombosis.

And someone else said he had heard the city council was going to erect a toll booth at the entrance to the Veale Gardens gay beat, such was the endless flow of Grab-a-Grub traffic.

'Just kidding,' he said, to nervous laughter.

Outside, it was raining hard, too hard to leave, and, to kill time, I said to Pete: 'Did you know, Birthday Boy, that the Trappist monks of France dig their own graves, a few spadefuls a day, to remind them of their mortality?'

'Buh-luddy hell,' Pete said, 'someone get me a shovel.'

6 June 2001

Try trusting a journalist

AS YOU READ THIS, my mother is flying to the US to attend the seventieth birthday party of a dear friend who happens to be related by marriage to Bill Gates – yes, that Bill Gates, the Microsoft billionaire.

She is staying at the Gates family compound in Seattle – not for the first time, either. Beyond that, I am not at liberty to reveal anything, on pain of maternal wrath.

You see, somewhere along the line, my mother, my very own mother, has learned to think twice before telling me much of interest for fear that I might repeat it. Me, her son, the journalist.

A certain amount of motherly trust seems to be lacking here, if I am not mistaken. Thank goodness I am not thin skinned.

True, most journalists would sell their grandmother's eye tooth for a good story, and a juicy tidbit of Gates gossip is not asking too much of a mum, surely? I can keep a confidence as well as the next person but, really, what's the point?

All I want is for her to reveal what life is like inside the Gates compound. But she either clams up entirely or – with a threatened 'Don't you ever repeat this!' – she offers something drearily obvious such as how the area is ringed by a security fence. Thanks, Mum.

She is not the only one who seems wary in my company, sad to say. I have lost count of the number of times people have said to me, 'Not for quoting, but ...' or 'You can't report this, but ...' or suchlike.

I mean, why bother to tell me stuff if it is not meant to be repeated? That's my job.

A colleague with another newspaper once interviewed Sir Donald Bradman and later wrote that The Don had told him something very, very important on condition that it not be revealed until after his death.

For a journalist to withhold such a gem is, I think, a breach of trust with the reader who expects to be told the facts, not to be teased with a nyah-nyah 'I know something you don't know.'

Bradman has since died and so far as I am aware, no startling revelation has yet emerged, so the whole episode is rather questionable, and most frustrating. I would not put it past The Don to have said something revealing – his inner thoughts about Greg Chappell would be interesting – and then claim confidentiality afterwards, as in: 'By the way, everything I just told you is off the record, okay?' No, not okay.

Merilyn the Barber tried the same line after telling me she sings and dances madly after a few drinks, to the extent that her son jokes that her photo is pinned up at a certain nightclub with the warning: 'Do not serve this woman.'

Had she not then said this was off the record, it would have slipped my mind immediately. But having been warned off, the urge to repeat it was uncontrollable, of course. So I just did.

Now, to work on my mother when she gets back.

15 August 2001

Life is a bowl of green bananas

MY POMMY MATE Stephen Tracey, whose health currently is as rickety as the English batting order, once told me that prolonged, heavy use of cocaine rots the bones and joints.

Which certainly puts the waiting list for hip replacements in a different light.

Mind, we happen to know someone, an old hippie now nearing sixty, who is in excellent physical condition considering how much cocaine he has snorted over the years. Our theory is he has ingested so many different chemicals they must have balanced each other out.

Stephen's spine is crumbling, not from cocaine but from cancer, and he is undergoing radiotherapy at the Memorial Hospital as you read this.

At home one morning, eternally optimistic of a turn-around in England's cricket fortunes, he put his foot on the side of the bath to dry between his toes.

Next thing he was in agony on the floor, a sliver of bone having sheared off a lower vertebrae and embedded itself in his sciatic nerve. He screamed a lot, he said.

Stephen then had to drag himself excruciatingly down five steps from the bathroom to the living room to ring his good friend Lyn, a nurse at Ashford. At this stage he thought he had a slipped disc.

Lyn duly turned up but Stephen lives upstairs in a secure building and she had no key. D'oh.

What followed was a slapstick routine of him, still lying on the floor, throwing the keys out the window, of them nearly falling through a grate, and then of tiny Lyn somehow levering a tottering Stephen down the stairs. He can laugh about it now.

In hospital, one scan led to another, and the medicos found the tumour. I learned about it while standing in The Duke and I immediately rang him on his mobile: 'Are you going to die?'

'I don't know yet.'

'I'll ring back later then.'

It did not come out as I intended and several people are not speaking to me. Not Stephen, though, who was as high as a kite on morphine at the time and does not remember the call.

His mates have since streamed into Memorial and Lyn says she has never heard so many grown men openly express their love for each other. They do when it matters.

When I went to see Stephen, he was lying in bed with his back to the door, his right hand inside his jocks having a good old scratch. He went to shake hands but I quickly gave him a peck on the forehead instead.

I told him how, at lunch the previous day, I had come across restaurateur Roger Moore – who seems to be aiming for some sort of heart bypass record – and had asked after his health.

'Let me put it this way,' Roger had said, 'I am not buying any green bananas.'

Stephen liked that and I left him two of the greenest bananas I could find. Love you, mate.

29 August 2001

Spring is sprung, the grass is rizz

THE MAGPIES in the parkland across the road have been at it since 2 am – the same thing every night for the past couple of months – restlessly carolling and celebrating the rising of their hormonal sap.

No creature awaits the end of winter with more impatience than the magpie.

The full moon is said to really get them going but I cannot tell the difference. Only a blustery wind seems to shut them up; apparently they are incapable of warbling and keeping their balance at the same time.

The swooping season cannot be far off, when we people are seen as fair game for attack rather than as possible friends. The maggie equivalent of an election campaign.

I love magpies. They make me smile with their cocky, bouncy personalities. To me, they are the sound of Australia – the Aussie bagpipes.

On the way to Mildura via Tailem Bend, Karoonda and so on – where a hand-painted sign reads 'Watermelons Next 2 Hours' – every few kilometres of roadside verge seems to be occupied by its own magpie family.

All told, there must be hundreds of them along the highway, living off a rich diet of roadkill, certainly sufficient to keep them plump and glistening.

Away behind the screen of trees on both sides of the road, desolate fields stretch to the horizon, good for wheat but not much else and not for native creatures such as maggies.

But the verges themselves, those thin strips of vegetation just a few metres wide, provide habitat for an extraordinarily diverse range of flora and fauna. Which just goes to show that, left alone, the Australia bush can get a toehold anywhere despite our blind interference.

Taken together, all those thousands of kilometres of country verges amount to a giant nature reserve, probably larger in total area than our biggest national park. Time to form a Friends of Roadside Nature Reserves.

The verges are also tree-lined corridors that the wildlife can use to follow around the country. 'As the crow flies' is wherever the road leads.

Back home, this morning's lemonwater dawn is so cold it takes your breath away but the maggies over the road sound as happy as larks. Er, magpies.

In a couple of hours, the parkland will offer the rich pickings of little girls in tracksuits and ponytails waiting to play hockey and be swooped. Absolute maggie's meat.

So why should I be warbling on about magpies like this? Because spring has sprung and four years have just ticked over since my last cigarette. Great.

Today I think I shall walk around with a box of gold stars to sprinkle wherever I go. Or, with a chortle, go and swoop someone.

5 September 2001

Squinting from the sidelines

IN THE AFTERMATH of the US terror, let me tell you a family anecdote.

On the day President John F. Kennedy was shot in Dallas, Texas, my father was not far away on a business trip in Fort Worth.

That night, terribly upset, he went to the home of a business acquaintance and was shocked to find that the family dinner quickly became a celebration of Kennedy's death, with lots of whooping and dancing.

There, in the Deep South, the US Civil War was still being waged and the murder of the Yankee president was a cause for joy, not grief, in this particular household.

The story has been gnawing away at me ever since the kamikaze attacks on New York and Washington, after the TV scenes of Palestinians celebrating in the streets immediately afterwards.

If only CNN had been around that night at Fort Worth.

But there we have it in a nutshell, confirmed on live TV: terrorism is something that Muslims inflict on Christians. How very, very comforting, in the eternal conflict over two imaginary friends.

Quickly the talkback radio was filled with other childish simplicities in which Muslims were typically portrayed as dirty, stupid, greedy, untrustworthy and violent. Aborigines must be appreciating the break.

Yep, our natural instinct is to put down those who are not part of our own tribe, to find comfort and security in our own type, be it a footy side or our own ethnic origins.

But here, at its most deplorable, talkback radio was the bigoted cheerleader for people who have never had an original thought in their heads. The Ditto Mob who sit in their taxis amid the verbal confetti, muttering: 'Ditto, yep, agree with everything he just said.' Ah, the joy of being a mob, of finding common purpose and outrage in their otherwise bleak lives.

Meantime, President George Bush Jnr – looking very junior indeed at times – kept sending out seductively simple messages such as let's bomb Afghanistan back to the Stone Age, which should take no time at all.

Or saying that we are now engaged in the first war of the twenty-first century. I wish he would stop saying that.

The US has always had a formidable will to please itself no matter what the consequences. In this case, in a vengeful mood, they have every right to exact just retribution against the 'enemy', whoever it is.

Of course the attacks on New York and Washington were inhumane and shocking, so much so that the exclamation mark has worn off my email keyboard. But beyond race, beyond religion, gender or anything else in a fracturing world, the glue that binds us together is our shared humanity. Hold that thought.

Right at the moment, sitting here with a detached sense of unreality, I am a fretting optimist about the future, not for the first time in my life.

Pessimists are right; optimists change the world.

26 September 2001

Thin blue line now Corporate Cop

CRUSTY OLD Bill Sutherland, a copper in the Port in the 1940s or 50s, would be grumbling in his grave if he knew how the new breed of cops was being trained these days.

Customer focus; continuous improvement; best practice models; quality management; respecting diversity; constructive feedback. The Corporate Cop.

Whatever next? Privatisation? A SAPol share float?

Bill, an alderman on the Woodville Council when I met him in the early 1980s, said he had maintained good order in the Port by taking the young hoods behind the wharf sheds, giving them a good thump behind the ear and no more was said about it. Constructive feedback indeed.

He told the story with a twinkle in his rheumy eyes so it was hard to know if he was telling the truth. He also made wooden toys for needy kids at Christmas.

Bill came to mind recently when I was sitting on a 'Policing and Professionalism' panel discussion at Fort Largs Police Academy, as part of a course for aspiring inspectors. Don't ask me why I was invited.

There were eleven sergeants – only one of whom was a woman, which is another issue – arguing the toss over ethical leadership: integrity, corruption, trust and power.

Here were cops angry at how people had been cast out of mental institutions and left to fend for themselves without proper support services, leaving the police to pick up the pieces.

Cops worrying about the community's loss of civil

liberties if politicians used the 'war against terrorism' as an excuse to restrict our freedoms. And anticipating the day when they would need to take a public profile in insisting that governments provided adequate services to achieve fairness and equity.

Not quite what I had expected.

At last count, there were 3600 active police officers in South Australia, give or take a cadet or two, compared to more than 6000 licensed security guards. Meaning personal or business security is available to those who can afford it, which rather leaves the rest of us on the other side of the chainmesh fence.

But extra police were not necessarily needed, according to our next inspectors. Better, they said, to provide the proper human services to intervene early and break the cycle of crime. All very encouraging.

At the same time, SAPol has a worrying high rate of staff turnover, with the average length of service only about six years. Presumably, many who leave are the bright young things whose career ambitions cannot be satisfied within the existing SAPol structure.

The worry, I suggested to a frosty reception, was the dead wood who would otherwise have remained sergeants might now be promoted to inspectors in order to fill the vacuum. Present company excepted, of course.

Afterwards I received a police mug which, the next time my place is broken into, I shall take to the local cop shop for a coffee and a reassuring chat about the philosophy of effective policing.

7 November 2001

We all have our crosses to bear

HANGING IN the dining room of the Catholic Archbishop's mansion on West Terrace is a portrait gallery of all the bishops who have ruled the roost over their Adelaide flock. Not exactly a rogues' gallery although among them is Bishop Shiel, the man who excommunicated Mary McKillop. Shiel's portrait is done in a flat, harsh style.

Also among them, on the east wall, is one of Leonard Faulkner, in musk pink, who has just retired after seventeen years as Adelaide's Archbishop. The face, painted toward the start of his term, is frozen in bewildered fear.

It was done by Archibald winner Robert Hannaford, who captured a simple country bloke startled by the spotlight, unable to explain quite how he was chosen for the top job or why, seized by self-doubt, and not appearing much to like having his portrait painted either. As a psychological insight, it has the haunting undertones of Edvard Munch's *The Scream*. Or of a boa constrictor having swallowed an elephant.

The first time I met Leonard Faulkner was at the media citations that the SA Catholic Church stages annually. Searching for small talk, I mentioned George Pell – Archbishop of Melbourne at the time and now in Sydney – who had refused to serve communion to open homosexuals.

The same Hannaford look of alarm froze His Grace's face and he moved quickly on. Neither struck by lightning nor turned into a pillar of salt, I counted myself lucky.

Every year since, I have attended the same awards and every year His Grace has said something like, 'We've met before, haven't we?', and I have just nodded and told him he was doing a great job and to keep it up.

Then, a couple of years ago, I was awarded a citation myself and we were photographed standing together, The Arch and me. Again, he had the same look of shocked bewilderment. Me too.

Leonard Faulkner made it his mission as Archbishop to reclaim the 80 per cent of baptised Catholics who have lapsed, me included. He set up neighbourhood groups known as Basic Ecclesial Communities, or BECs, whose members personally visit people who do not attend Mass and invite them back into parish life. No one has knocked on my door, thank God.

Hardly controversial stuff given the missionary evange-lisation of the Catholic Church down the ages, but Archbishop Faulkner suddenly found himself targeted by the Catholic Right. The BECs, through the Right's distorted lens, were supposed to be a dangerous example of 'neo-Marxist liberation theology'. They even had spies in parish churches to dob on any backsliding.

I happen to think Archbishop Faulkner is a humble, holy man with no ambition other than to serve his God. He certainly is no neo-Marxist revolutionary, or no more so than Jesus Christ was.

In any event, Leonard Faulkner gets my vote as Personage of the Year 2001 to give him his due, and also to acknowledge his church's leading role in exposing the government's racist treatment of asylum seekers and the appalling conditions at the Woomera detention centre.

Old priests never die, they live forever.

12 December 2001

Doc leaves as a winner

BECAUSE I WAS off doing something else, I never heard that Doc had died. I missed his funeral and, worse, missed his wake in The Duke, which everyone said did him proud.

I last saw him in mid-December after hearing from winemaker Brian Barry, one of his punting mates, that he had been hospitalised with a burst stomach ulcer. That should put a hole in your profits, I told Brian, knowing how much Doc enjoyed a Barry red.

'I don't know about that,' Brian smiled and, sure enough, when I tracked down the Doc next day in the members' bar, he was hunched over in pain, white as a sheet, with a glass of red on the bar.

I chided him and he greeted me with 'Ah, the Gutter Press has arrived!' as he always did, and we chatted briefly before I moved on. He did not look well.

He died of a heart attack at 4 am on Boxing Day after having told various people he would not be seeing them again after Christmas. Quite a premonition. I wish I had known because I would have run a book.

Doc was the local dentist serving the Beirut corner of the city. The fang farrier, as Ron 'The Rat' Menzies called him. Ron's wife Gwen was his dental assistant. Doc marked fifty years as a dentist last October, which probably made him the oldest practising dentist in South Australia. He mostly limited his surgery to mornings although some starts were too early for him.

My mate Lance tells of the time he went in to have a crown fitted. Lying back in the chair with his eyes shut tight and Doc leaning lightly on his shoulder, he heard the 'ting … ting … ting-tink-tinktinktink' of something falling on the floor. The weight on Lance's shoulder gradually felt heavier and next Doc's snoring began. The crown lay on the floor.

For all that, Doc was said to be a good dentist who bulk billed – unheard of in my experience – and he looked after the teeth of all and sundry including Adelaide's best known madam, Stormy Summers.

After morning surgery, he would join his mate Louis at The Duke and get on the punt. Some of my fondest memories are of them nattering over the form guide, with Sky Racing on the overhead TV and Doc offering free advice on how to fix Australia's political system.

For example, he insisted the ALP had abandoned its roots and no longer deserved his vote. Given he had sympathy for some of One Nation's rattier notions, it was hard to imagine which Labor Party he was talking about. We argued passionately and pleasurably.

Ron and Gwen went to see him lying in state at the funeral parlour. Ron told me afterwards he wished he had taken a camera. 'Mate, they tubbed him up beautifully, they really did.'

Gwen, as she always did, checked the back of Doc's collar to make sure it was turned down properly and left a TAB bet sticking out his breast pocket for Thanks A Bundle, which was due to run later that day.

And the damn thing won.

23 January 2002

Heat does odd things

ON GOOD AUTHORITY, I understand that in the early years at Elizabeth, whenever the hot northerlies blew, whole families would set up camp in the Casualty section of the Lyell McEwin Hospital because it was the only public place locally with air conditioning.

There, amid the groans and broken bones, they picnicked on cucumber sandwiches and lemonade while waiting for the cool change to come and they could finally go home. I suppose the entertainment value was no different than going to a violent movie today, and it was free.

Most places are air conditioned now. Shopping centres could not exist without it but sometimes, like it or not, we still have to go out in the heat.

Last month, as a guest of AQ Print, I watched the Tour Down Under at Nuriootpa in 40 degree heat. Better to be drinking cold beer than riding a bike, let me tell you.

The Tanunda Town Band entertained the crowd and they seemed to be playing along merrily enough until, one of the three girl timpanists told me, all the brass instruments had gone out of tune in the heat.

Yes, it has been that kind of summer, one day brass monkey weather, the next you cannot keep a brass band in tune. And I had been wondering why the trombonist kept dipping his mouthpiece in a glass of chilled white wine.

As for the Timpani Trio, whenever their talents were not required, such as during 'Boogie Woogie Bugle Boy of Company B', they stepped to the front of the band and performed a Spice Girls dance routine, which was different. Very different.

The heat can produce strange effects. At home later, needing a saline drip, I spent fully five minutes staring at the face of the barometer before realising it would not tell me the time.

Maybe it was the paint fumes. You see, Dante the Painter had been working on my place. Dante – what else would an Italian painter be called? – spent a lot of time filling cracks in the walls, as you have to do in Adelaide, before applying the paint.

One hot afternoon I returned home to find him as red as a Ferrari. He had two fan heaters going full blast to speed up the drying process for the crack filler and it must have been at least 45 degrees.

I had to admire his dedication, even if he was costing me a fortune in power.

Speaking of which, while Dante was still there I asked Tom the Electrician to install an overhead combination heater/fan in the bathroom. A fairly simple task, one would have thought.

But no, there are now two extractor fans in the bathroom, a hard-wired smoke detector, four extra power points in the bedroom, more switches in the hall than I know what to do with and a huge bill that included seven hours' labour.

I should never have left them together in the heat.

13 February 2002

Her Maj, The Prez and me

AT SEVENTY-FIVE, my mother is the same age as the Queen and my father was the same vintage as Prince Phillip – compelling evidence as a child of a mystical link between the Ryans and the Royal Family, to the extent that I confidently expected the Queen to pop in any time for a cuppa.

She never showed up and the psychological damage may later have driven me into the arms of the Republican movement. You never know.

Yet somehow or another, I was on the guest list at last week's State Dinner for QEII at the Festival Centre – who compiles these lists anyway? – and I rang my mother beforehand to ask if she had any message for Her Maj?

'Tell her not to forget the telegram.' Likely as not, given they both appear to be in robust health, they will be swapping telegrams at 100.

Security being what it is these days, I got nowhere near close enough to QEII to give her the message. From the back, I could not even see her tiara until she stood up to speak.

She read out one of those standard royal speeches about how great we Australians are, padded out with statements of the bleeding obvious such as 'the way Australia evolves over the next fifty years is in your hands'. Being the royal speechwriter must be a special kind of hell.

A couple of nights earlier, in a big week, I also had 'An Evening with President Clinton', at the Entertainment Centre. I asked my mother if she had any messages for Bill?

'No, but keep your distance. You do not need any more bad habits.' I do not even smoke cigars.

I was a lot closer to The Prez than I was to Her Maj, within lunging distance in fact at the next table. Alongside me was Doug, 'The Presidential Aide' according to his card, who was liverish about a story in the *Australian* which had said Clinton commanded a routine fee of $300,000 per speech and he had been going around Australia giving the same speech.

Doug quoted The President as saying: 'If that's what I am getting paid, we need to have a quiet word with my agent.' Doug said the fee was not even a third of $300,000 – crumbs for someone with post-Monica legal bills.

The official introductions kept saying what an honour and a privilege it was to have Bill in town. But the departing Premier Rob Kerin trumped everyone by saying: 'We are in awe of what you have done.' On that we are unanimous – even my mother agrees.

Next came a stand-up comic but a lot of his best local jokes – the ones about Alan Bond, Harold Holt and Kerry Packer – had to be explained to The Prez through the host Gerald McGrath whispering in his ear. However, a line about Dolly Parton being able to breastfeed all of China immediately cracked him up.

With his remarkable blue-grey bouffant hair, he was the celebrity turn alright, whether talking about global warming, AIDS, 'East T'Moor', or Albert Bensimon's Hoo-Ha Party and the peculiarities of the Australian political system. He should talk; Doug was from Florida.

Quite a coup, though, having both President Clinton and Queen Elizabeth as headline acts in this year's Fringe.

6 March 2002

My Wingfield vision splendid

WHAT ADELAIDE NEEDS is a new theme park that will make us different, something beyond Magic Mountain, more cutting edge than the Haigh's chocolate factory and more entertaining than the National Wine Centre. Already I have a vision for Wingfield Tip.

Think about it: The tip is due to close in 2004 when it reaches a height of 27 metres, which is only 700 metres lower than Mt Lofty. Hardly any difference at all on the global scale of mountains.

So let's keep dumping our rubbish there, and dumping and dumping and not stop until the tip reaches a hundred times higher at 2700 metres, taller even than Mt Kosciuszko.

It can be our contribution to the International Year of the Mountain.

Let's create our very own Mt Wingfield – an unrivalled theme park offering snowfields, mountain climbing, a reliable water supply, wind power and methane production to meet our energy needs for centuries.

Okay, okay, I'm okay, I'm okay ... Actually my favourite Adelaide theme park is the zoo, which I visit at isolated intervals even though I feel guilty about keeping animals captive.

Adelaide Zoo has its charms and for some reason I am always drawn to the enclosure containing the solitary male orangutan, with the marvellous scientific name *pongo pygmaeus abeli* and the sign that says it all: 'No, I am not lonely.'

Quite. So why look like a jilted lover in self-imposed exile?

Next, I always check the regent honeyeaters to make sure they are still there, just in case, to see if the mystery of their love lives has finally been solved.

Their cage sign cryptically reads: 'A mystery surrounds the disappearance of most regent honeyeaters after the breeding season'. That's all. I find it hard to believe David Attenborough does not know the answer by now.

The zoo is full of all sorts of improbable human creatures, too. Such as the mum I saw who deliberately tried to scare her whimpering toddler son with: 'Look at the baboon, go on, get up close to the window, closer, ooh, you're not scared, are ya?'

Scared enough for the kid to have nightmares and grow up to be a sooky Crows supporter with a trembling bottom lip. Heh-heh.

The zoo is also a favourite spot for sad dads with weekend access to the kids; a gathering of Jasons and Jades, baseball hats on backwards, who are so familiar with the place by now they almost know the Barbary sheep on first name terms.

Still, better for them to be here than spending Sunday arvo at the pub, which is where dad likes to spend his spare time on the punt. And where else can kids watch tammars in their mock rainforest having sexual union for less than the price of a cinema ticket?

Meantime, glimpsed through the trees, glinting in the sun, a snow-capped Mt Wingfield rises above the plain ...

27 March 2002

Drug strategy futile farce

IN MY SOLITARY YEAR of studying Applied Chemistry in 1970, it dawned on me that lysergic acid diethylamide was almost easier to make than to say – that's LSD to you and me, baby, the chemical of psychedelic dreams.

Our lecturer never actually taught us how to make LSD but its chemical formula was plain to see and, even for a plodding first year student like me, the production process could be deduced quite easily.

Yet I never made LSD for much the same reason that I never tried it either, or heroin, or cocaine or any of the so-called designer drugs such as amphetamines or ecstasy.

Cowardice.

No promise of chemically induced pleasure could overcome my fear of taking something that had been blended in someone's back shed and adulterated with whatever else happened to be handy.

My job eventually brought me into contact with the real life narcotics industry – I use the word 'industry' quite deliberately – and I met people who were later to die of drug overdoses, including a cousin whose death broke everyone's heart and crushed the fun out of her parents.

One time, my place was broken into by a heroin addict and his prostitute girlfriend who stole my laptop and VCR to fund their habits, and he died of an overdose not long afterwards. So it goes.

For all that, I have reached the stage now where I think all drugs should be legalised. All drugs. I must be out of my mind suggesting such a thing but to my way of thinking, the minute a drug is made illegal, the black market booms and the drug-crime cycle begins.

And then the rest of the 'drug industry' clunks into gear – police, health and welfare workers, lawyers and politicians, judges and jailers – all at a national cost of hundreds of millions of dollars. A ship of fools.

Not only is the 'war on drugs' ineffective, it is a futile waste of money, scandalously so given the way the 'war' is used for self-serving ends by our politicians.

Even the head of the National Crime Authority has admitted the drug war is lost, which rather begs the question: Why we are persisting with a policy that is such an expensive failure? Makes no sense to me.

Anyone who suggests that cracking down harder on drugs is the answer must be suffering delusions of denial. The drug producers and smugglers love prohibition because it increases their profit margins without much increasing their risks of capture.

Some people will try drugs, some won't, but very few, say no more than two per cent, will become problem addicts. Decriminalising hard drugs will make no difference to the addiction rate.

The addicts need to be treated as if they have a medical condition not a criminal one, in clean, supervised heroin injecting rooms, if needs be.

Premier Mike Rann has promised to hold a drug summit in June, which is all well and good. But, as I understand it, heroin injecting rooms will not be on the agenda. Why not, Mike?

24 April 2002

When T.A. always served you right

THE BEST HEADWAITER I ever saw in action was Terry Armstrong from the old Braested, on Greenhill Road, when it was still a restaurant in the 1980s and not the aged care home it has become.

Everyone knew him as T.A. He remembered all the guests' names and food preferences; always walked clockwise around a table, leading with the left foot and serving from the right; and never carried more than three plates, all balanced on one arm if necessary to leave the other hand free to arrange a guest's napkin.

T.A. was a combination of relaxed charm and professional perfection. Carer, adviser and entertainer. T.A. had the gift. He also used to camp it up a bit.

One of his naughty tricks was to go around a matronly table of eight serving each in turn until, on reaching the guest of honour – perhaps the grande dame celebrating her eightieth birthday – he would release a wind-up toy that had been hidden in his palm.

Ho-ho, the cackles of horror and delight as a little plastic willy on two feet waddled across the table. I think it was T.A. who told me that a person who is nice to you but rude to the waiter is not a nice person.

But there are limits, T.A. Such as the lunch I had recently with a cop and a publican at a newish city restaurant where we had three young waitresses always in our face like a revolving door, more like spruikers, repeatedly interrupting the conversation to get our orders out of the way.

'The duck breast? Fabulous choice, sir – that's just what

I would have ordered! ... Oh, yes, the lamb is fabulous, too, but best slightly underdone, yes, even if it does turn your stomach ... The riesling is a favourite of mine, sir, one of Wolf Blass's best vintages. Fabulous.'

With the meal over and an unfinished bottle of wine on the sideboard, suddenly we became invisible and I had to help myself to the wine while the girls milled around elsewhere chewing their hair ends. When the matron d' finally hove into view, she had the gall to say: 'You poured that in the wrong glass.' A corked tongue.

This is not a restaurant review, lucky for them. Instead, I left no tip. I will not return there and will happily repeat the name to anyone who asks.

I blame the speed-eating trend – 'I want something to eat and I want it NOW!' – the serve yourself buffet, the all day breakfast, the table of eight who order coffees and start complaining if they do not arrive within a minute.

Which rather begs the question: which is more important, the food or the service? I have returned to restaurants where the food was ordinary if the service was good; rarely, however, have I bothered to return when the service was slovenly or pushy, no matter how good the food.

I do not remember any particular dishes at Braested but I do have happy memories of T.A. Presumably he has retired. I have not seen him for years but some time ago, second or third hand, I heard that he wanted to catch up for old time's sake. But his phone number somehow went missing and nothing eventuated.

Ring me, T.A., and we will lunch and lament the decline in service standards.

15 June 2002

Sorry is not the only word for it

FOR OLD TIME'S SAKE, John Gregory had thought up a special menu of such delicacies as Mimili Mains – 'freshly opened tin of curried sausages in cheesy sauce spaghetti'; and Pipalyatjara Dessert – 'freshly thawed frozen bread and margarine with live honey ants'.

A nice touch for a reunion lunch with our Welsh mate Taffy, who I first met on a trip with John to the Pitjantjatjara Lands in 1978 when Taffy was a school principal there. John was president of the Institute of Teachers at the time and, for his sins, now heads the renamed Australian Education Union in South Australia. Some people never learn.

Taffy spent five years in the Pit Lands and the experience changed him, as it would. He last went back three years ago to show some overseas friends where he had lived but could not find the house.

What he did find deeply distressed him – the social and physical devastation – and he could hardly speak about it over lunch. He said petrol sniffing was out of control.

It was bad enough back in 1978. We recalled how, on the night before John and I had arrived, a teacher aide's caravan had caught fire. The aide had grabbed the hose but whole sections were missing where the sniffers had chopped out lengths to use as petrol siphons. The caravan was gutted.

A white teacher there had mentioned to me how it was easier to leave your petrol cap unlocked otherwise the sniffers would use a star dropper to put a hole in the fuel tank. Taffy, a good and decent man, always kept his petrol cap switches to silver grey under stress and then to gold in the sunlight. Only in America;

- women's tights – in the US again – which release subtle amounts of moisturiser onto the legs all day. Peeling them off at night must feel dreadful;
- Nuku Nuku Ashiyu powder, from Japan. Added to bathwater, it becomes a gel that is said to hold the heat longer. A special dissolving agent must be added to turn it back to liquid. Ugh;
- Phota Lite glow-in-the-dark powder, which contains the same enzyme responsible for a firefly's light. Described by the Japanese makers as a 'fun drink additive', try slipping some into your best mate's beer for a laugh.

Ah, human progress. Closer to home, another example that irks me is the Gillette Mach3 Triple Blade 'shaving system' – blatant merchandising that has little to do with offering an innovative product. Whatever next, Gillette – four blades, five, nine?

Sitting here with a beer watching the mousetrap in the corner behind the telly, no mouse, dead or alive, has made its appearance for over a week now. Perhaps the mouse recognises the trap for what it is, even if other people can't. Or maybe it prefers crunchy peanut butter.

Nothing less than the body of a dead mouse will satisfy me, however, and I have a good supply of beer in the fridge to wait it out.

The US essayist Ralph Waldo Emerson almost said: If a man can build a better mousetrap, the world will beat a path to his door. But not mice, it seems.

24 July 2002

Try explaining it to the kids

One Saturday morning a while ago in the Barossa Valley, I was involved in a 'hypothetical' organised by the Law Society on the detention of asylum seekers at Gulag Woomera and shortly after at Gulag Baxter.

Also on the panel were academics, lawyers, the clergy, officers from the Department of Immigration and Multicultural Affairs (DIMA) and Liberal MHR Christopher Pyne, who was Immigration Minister Philip Ruddock for the occasion.

Pyne made a poor Ruddock – far too animated and colourful, giving as good as he got with derisory asides at the 'hysterical rhetoric of the Feminazis' on the panel.

To be fair on Pyne, only Ruddock can do Ruddock, wearing an Amnesty lapel pin and doing his doublespeak routine, the point of which seems to make the asylum debate so boring that people will not be tempted to think too deeply about it. Ruddock also proves that having hooded brown eyes does not necessarily mean you are well connected with the Taliban.

Pyne had to leave early, pity, after which the DIMA officers, sentiment running against them, were given a few uncomfortable moments and did not hang around for lunch.

Asked if the fence around Baxter would be electrified, one officer seemed most offended and said, no, the technical term was 'energised' – a subtlety worth remembering as you fizz and crackle upon the wire.

As for breaches of human rights, the same officer said DIMA, in support of free speech, had provided cardboard on which the Woomera detainees could make protest signs. So there.

My hypothetical dilemma, posing as a journalist, was to be told by a redneck editor that a Catholic priest harbouring Woomera escapees in his Adelaide presbytery would be raided by the police that evening. The priest was a close friend of mine. What to do?

What a coincidence, I said, for this very evening the priest and I were going out to dinner, or would be now.

There was also some hypothetical banter about journalists at a Woomera detention centre riot being knocked down in a melee of pro bono lawyers seeking publicity; and of the 'Dob in an Escapee' campaign run by the redneck editor – first prize, a family trip to Christmas Island in a leaky boat.

Much more seriously, the citizenry has become disconnected from politics for all sorts of reasons – but when did we become indifferent to the fate of helpless people and insensitive to their ill-treatment?

Wincing at lip sewing and suicidal kids, we offer a tut-tutting, dismissive shake of the head at refugees behaving badly but what else can you expect of extremists? Extremist Australians, I mean.

Faced with a supposed invasion of, er, which minority is it this time – Muslims? – democracy can be a dictatorship of the majority.

History is said to be a chronicle of what ought not to have happened. The future will bear down hard on us for what we ought to have done and did not do in our treatment of asylum seekers.

31 July 2002

This time, Ken, with feeling

KEN BARNES – mornin', Ken – rings me from time to time to pass on his compliments when I write something he likes. He has more than a passing interest in my columns because he is a volunteer for the Royal Society for the Blind and he reads his local Messenger onto tape for RSB clients.

For the blind, it means Ken's soft English accent is me. They have an impression of me through Ken and, thanks to him, they may consider me to be beautiful, strong, graceful and sociable.

Sadly, I am nothing like it but Ken undoubtedly makes me sound more cultured than I really am, for which I am grateful to him.

I never write with anyone particular in mind but, knowing Ken will have to read my column later, I try to keep out swear words and tone down any criticism of English sporting failures, which are many.

Yes, I do have the power to put words into Ken's mouth, which he must find unsettling at times, but then I have to rely on his emphasis and intonation to convey the sense of what I have written.

You would like Ken. He used to be a compositor at Messenger Press, typesetting headlines letter by letter, so having him read the paper aloud has a nice link to an earlier, less complicated time.

In a previous life he was also a member of the original BBC recording team on *The Goons*, a show dedicated to non-sensical plays on words if ever there was one.

He would probably enjoy an old advertising mate of mine who, among his crimes of illiteracy, has spoken of creeping ivory on the garden wall, an immaculate contraption and his vagina pills, er, angina pills. Sorry for making you read that, Ken. Heh-heh.

My mate's blurred speech also includes the Walk for the Dole scheme, saying antidote when he means anecdote and problems with the word superfluous, as in 'as superfluous as a seat on a chariot'. He says suferpluous.

He is tremendous fun to play Scrabble with.

Can you do an Irish accent, Ken? Then you might produce something that sounds like 'a liar and a barrister are one and the same'. Which may well be true in some cases but is substantially different to saying 'a lawyer and a barrister'.

The other evening, half listening to the TV headlines in the other room, I was more than a little surprised to hear an item about a rape crisis and ABC nudes.

Suddenly paying much closer attention, the story was about rate rises on the ABC news. Enjoy that, Ken?

Someone once said to me: 'I thought that column was good until I found out you wrote it.' Quite.

If you happen to enjoy what I write, don't spoil it by wishing to meet me in person. Speak to Ken instead, a lovely chap.

I enjoy the thought of Ken being my public voice. Better him than me.

Another nice read, thanks, Ken.

7 August 2002

Great glory awaits us

POGROMS, JIHADS, ethnic cleansings, Inquisitions and Crusades – one could be forgiven for asking did God really intend to establish religion?

Something dark sits at the heart of organised religion, something inherently intolerant, that leads to evil, slaughter and barbarism. A too human darkness.

The trouble is every religion rests on an absolute belief in its own superiority and the divine right to impose its version of the truth upon others.

Never mind which truth because in the world of religion no connection necessarily exists between what is true and what is believed to be true. Faith is the act of knowing something to be untrue and still believing it.

True, many people need and depend on religion to get them through this life and onto the next. Good luck to them.

Me, I placed more trust in the epigrams that used to appear on old MTT bus tickets.

Sorry about the outburst of righteous indignation here but you can blame State Attorney General Michael Atkinson and his whacky idea to legislate to ensure that no one can be discriminated against on the basis of his or her religion.

Michael, Michael ... whatever possessed you? Did your mother not warn you about discussing politics and religion in polite company?

I want to be free to set my sights on cults such as the Scientologists, or to take aim at religion generally, and do not want Michael Atkinson blocking my view.

In my experience, religions, especially the crackpot ones,

are more than capable of defending themselves and attacking debunkers without needing State intervention on their behalf.

Even Catholicism – my lapsed religion, a religion of mostly elderly women – generally has a good sense of humour about itself. Beset with all sorts of problems such as declining congregations and very few priests left to serve them, only a Catholic could quip: Will the last priest to leave please extinguish the candles?

Of course, people with different religious beliefs should not be vilified but that is not the same as racism or sexism, which are matters of fact not faith.

A quick aside: I recently heard a gay man rail against what he called the 'three evil-isms: racism, sexism and homophobia'. Uh-huh.

God, I hope blasphemy prosecutions no longer occur in this State. My lawyer says it is unlikely but not impossible.

Once, in the old Judaic tradition, misusing the name of God was blasphemy and the penalty was stoning to death. In the supreme irony, Jesus's assertion of his divine nature was blasphemous and led to his execution.

Does blasphemy apply only to a Christian God in Australia or is the privileged protection extended to Islam as well? No, it does not.

Look, the greatest freedom is to be allowed to be yourself, free to find personal fulfilment, and if people need religion in that quest, absolutely tremendous.

But I put 'atheist' on the last Census. If I guessed wrong, the consequences for me in the hereafter no doubt will be dreadful.

You take your chances in this life, as well as in the next.

14 August 2002

Scratching at the surface

BY THE TIME I drove into Broken Hill in the topaz light, the late sun glinting off the gravestones on the left, the cyst was draining poison across my shoulders and up the sides of my neck. Even my earlobes hurt.

Typical. Take a few days off to relax and travel, and a cyst the size of a cricket ball erupts on the back of your neck. Thanks.

That first night, seeking pain relief, I drank beer in the nearest pub and chatted footy to the nuggetty old locals with Brylcreemed hair and saltbush sprouting from their ears.

Broken Hill worries about itself. The day's *Barrier Daily Truth* had news about the ageing and declining population; of government benefits being the most common form of local income; of having one of the highest youth suicide rates in the country; and of clubs having to import 'Adelaide DJs' as headline acts. Thank God for footy.

By chance, the New South Wales Governor, Marie Bashir, was visiting Broken Hill at the same time, and we were staying in the same hotel. She said she liked the hotel's four-grain bread. I would like to have challenged her to a game of billiards except I could not raise my sore neck high enough to get a line of sight at the balls.

The next morning, feeling worse if possible, I drove to Silverton and peered across the Mundi Mundi plain, the edge of the world. Mundi Mundi is supposed to mean 'a place where there is much permanent water'. A joke, surely? The winter flies were a pest that I constantly had to wave away until I absent-mindedly slapped at one on my neck. The scream must have reached Arkaroola.

Something had to be done, so I went to the Broken Hill Base Hospital in search of drugs, for which I would have killed by that stage. 'This hospital will not tolerate AGGRESSIVE BEHAVIOUR and supports police intervention' said the emergency department sign. Thanks for the warning.

The doctor at reception said: 'Oh, I see, it's your eye.'

'Huh?'

'Your right eye is inflamed.'

'Impressed as I am by your quick diagnosis, the problem is my neck. I can live with a terrigium but not a cyst.'

A different doctor eventually saw me and we had a chat about Magnoplasm and molasses and other home remedies, and whether or not the cyst should be lanced.

He thought not, and sent me along to the hospital pharmacy for antibiotics, where the girl asked: 'Do you have a pensioner card?' No, I bloody well do not, and she rapidly gave me the drug for $15.40, which was cheaper than the all-you-can-eat buffet at the Musicians' Club that night.

Later in my hotel room, standing up from the toilet faster than my stiff neck allowed my head to rise, I banged my skull on the towel rail and took a piece out of my scalp. Ow ow ow. Taking extra painkillers and the antibiotics as prescribed and not wishing to risk any further injury, I went early to bed.

On Central TV at 8.22, a giant bilby was being tucked into bed, just like Fat Cat on Channel 10 in the 1970s, and the voice-over said: 'Goodnight, Boys and Girls.'

'Goodnight, Mr Bilby,' I murmured, and fell into a drugged dream of hard, desert rain on corrugated iron houses.

21 August 2002

11 hours eating Killer Pythons

THIS SATURDAY, come hell and high water, bantamweight Verity Edwards will compete in the Hawaiian Ironman, a combined 225 kilometres of swimming, cycling and running in one day.

Verity, a twenty-something Messenger journalist, expects the whole thing to take her about eleven hours to finish, by about 6 pm Hawaiian time. The cut-off is midnight, so she has some time up her, er, singlet.

The Hawaiian Ironman – there is no Ironwoman – was first staged on the island of Oahu, named after the oh-ah-oow noise that tri-athletes made crossing a lava field in the scorching sun, as they really do in this event.

The swim leg is 3.9 kilometres, equivalent to swimming between Henley and Grange jetties twice. I know someone, not Verity, who has done the annual Henley-to-Grange swim twice, both times while pregnant. The extra buoyancy apparently helps.

The bike leg is 180 kilometres, the same as from Woodville to Nuriootpa and back. 'Nigel's parents live at Nuriootpa,' Verity said after a training ride, 'so when we get to the halfway mark we sit down for fifteen minutes and eat homemade chocolate cake and lamingtons. If you can't eat chocolate cake when you're riding 180 kilometres, when can you?' Quite.

In a recent Hawaiian Ironman, the side winds roared over the lava field so fiercely that some competitors were knocked off their bikes. Should the wind blow again this year, Verity, all 52 kilograms of her, will be tossed across to the next island.

The final leg is a marathon run of 42.2 kilometres, or about 3000 jelly snakes in Verity's training regime. She carries snakes with her for the sugar hit but thinks she will take carbohydrate gels during the event itself.

She knows lots about nutrition now. I mentioned that we were told at school never to drink water before playing football because it would cause stomach cramps. Same thing with eating food inside half an hour of a swim.

Both old wives' tales, said Verity. Imagine how damned good I would have been with water.

She has spent twelve months preparing for this weekend's race. I asked how much weight she had lost in hard training and she said, not much, maybe a kilogram, because the fat had been converted into muscle. My excuse, too.

She certainly looked great before leaving for Hawaii last week, positively glowing in fact, no blisters, trim and taut, although she said she was feeling a bit tired from the training. Have another Killer Python, Verity.

Her partner, Nigel, did the Hawaiian Ironman in 2000. After he'd run all day in the sun, Verity said, the unburnt silhouette of the painted numbers on his arms and legs could still be seen weeks later. I do hope she gets a nice number.

As it happens, another friend of mine, a woman of middling years, is doing the New York marathon next month. What has got into these women?

Mind, she is going to walk the course, not run it, and afterwards she has an apartment to herself in the extremely exclusive Trump Towers where she can recover before going shopping on Fifth Ave.

Life for an elite athlete is hell.

16 October 2002

Sting numbs horse sense

PEACHES, I really like, and nec-
tarines and plums, too, but not apricots – fresh, preserved or as jam – no
way Jose, or Simon.

As a kid, every backyard seemed to have an apricot tree
in it and the smell of summer for me is still the sickly sweet
smell of apricots rotting in the hot sun, maggot infested
and squishy underfoot.

Yuck, the smell hit me again just by thinking about it.

The other day I was at a housewarming and Simon T.,
one of the guests, mentioned that the apricot tree in his
backyard at Parkside had set no fruit this year. Ho-hum,
Simon, diddums.

But when he blamed it on urban consolidation – uh-huh –
I was, you might say, a lot more intrigued.

Simon said he had been inspecting the tree that very
morning and wondering why there were no apricots when it
struck him ... he had seen no bees either this season.

Given that fruit trees needed bees for pollination, he
believed the two might be linked. Quite possibly.

Assuming there was indeed a bee shortage, I suggested
it might have been too cold for them, although that was a
guess. Frost perhaps? Pesticide? Or maybe the drought was
to blame although I could not think why.

I also threw in an aside about noticing some European
wasps floating around my bedroom window last week,
thinking the wasps might have driven away the bees.

But Simon was not to be distracted. He thought the lack
of bees had something to do with all the old houses being

demolished to make way for the crowds of neo-Tuscan units that kept popping up everywhere.

He said the bees no longer had roof spaces or sheltered eaves in which to build their hives, therefore no bees. Marginally possible, I supposed, though rather stretching it a bit.

Matthew M., who had been standing there listening only because we were blocking his access to the Esky, said there were plenty of bees at his place at Glengowrie.

No bees at Parkside but lots at Glengowrie – hmmm, perhaps they were migrating towards the coast as they grew older, the same as humans. Obviously heading for retirement at Brighton. Or were they aspirational bees making for Holdfast Shores?

Matthew worried about the bees stinging his little boys. I told him clearly the best way to deter bees was to plant an apricot tree, just ask Simon. We could have gone on like this all afternoon but fortunately a cold wind sprang up and I went home.

The bees were still playing on my mind a couple of days later when I was seeking divine guidance, the tips of strangers, signs in the shape of clouds, or whatever, to try to pick the winner of the Melbourne Cup.

Obviously all the omens pointed to Beekeeper, so I backed it for a win and a place, and threw in Miss Meliss as well because the name Melissa was Greek for 'honey'.

Beekeeper ran third, which at least meant I got some of my money back. The winner Media Puzzle was too obvious for someone in my job and I had been stung before by going on gut feel.

13 November 2002

Possum War's final solution

NOW IS THE TIME of the year when the conversation around countless backyard barbies turns to the never-ending Great Possum War of Adelaide.

Many neighbourhoods have been under siege for years. Possums squabble inside the roofs; ceilings develop unspeakable stains and odours; and gardens are stripped of their flowers and new growth.

One particular grapevine has not borne fruit for five years because the possums keep eating the new leaf tips. At her wit's end, the householder has tried everything from trapping, to blocking every entry point in the roof, to now boiling quassia chips and spraying the liquid around to dissuade them.

Quassia is said to be as bitter as bitter can be and, since Fauna Rescue says it is a natural pesticide and a poison, I will take their word for it. Herbal healers also claim quassia stimulates the appetite, promotes bile flow, expels thread-worms, treats malaria and dysentery and even helps people to quit alcohol. Possums do not know what they are missing.

Even more bitterly, possums have the power to divide people who would otherwise be good neighbours. One side wants the possums removed and good riddance; the other puts up feeding boxes which only encourages them.

Oh, yes, tears have been shed before bedtime and, owing to the possums, not much sleep is to be had afterwards.

People go to desperate lengths. A friend caught three possums in his roof, stuffed them live into a hessian bag, and took them on the bus to Cobbler's Creek, beyond Tea

Tree Gully, where they were released to face certain death at the hands of other possums.

On the way there, he showed some schoolkids on the bus what he had in the bag and they oohed and aahed at how cute they were. If only they knew what the nice man was doing.

Another friend, a respectable company director for most of the time, told me over a barbecued chop that he had shot the possums in his backyard gum trees.

He loaded a shotgun with Z-shot, fitted a silencer so the neighbours would not become alarmed, and even had a laser sight with a red spot to take aim in the dark.

It seemed a bit over the top to me but certainly showed how passionate people could become with possums.

Having seen a possum stand its ground against a cat, I told Gunsmoke I would back a possum against a cat any time. Maybe, he said, but not against a Rhodesian Ridgeback which he owned – a very serious possum dog indeed.

Fauna Rescue has all sorts of advice on how to deal with possums such as installing a one-way flap in your roof; erecting tree boxes and feeding platforms; pruning to leave a gap between the roof and trees; putting metal collars around tree trunks; installing lights in the garden and in the ceiling; and the list goes on.

None of them really works.

The best way of handling the problem is possum ragout. Master chef Cheong Liew makes a good one at the Hilton although, let it be firmly noted, he obtains the possums from Tasmania.

www.faunarescue.org.au

20 November 2002

Ying Chow praise hard to swallow

NEVER ONE to exaggerate unless my life depended on it, I was astonished the other day to read that Ying Chow had been declared the 'world's best Chinese restaurant'.

The world's noisiest restaurant, quite possibly, but the notion that Ying Chow – the pokey little place on Gouger Street – is the very best of its type anywhere on the globe, including China, is too absurd for words.

Yet, according to a piece in the *Age*, the 'Food & Wine' magazine in the US – a publishing offshoot of American Express – named it No.1.

Having eaten occasionally at Ying Chow, I emailed the F&W editor Dana Cowin, in New York, to ask if she was being serious or should we take it with a pinch of monosodium glutamate? I await her response.

Not that I am necessarily bagging Ying Chow but the praise is such an exaggeration, so beyond reason, that the place cannot possibly live up to unfair expectations. They must be cursing their Chinese luck.

The basis of all exaggeration is the three words, good, better, best. Or, as is often the case in news stories, bad, worse, worst.

Exaggeration is an occupational hazard in journalism. Governments are 'slammed' by a 'huge backlash' of voters and unions warn of 'massive job losses'.

Exaggeration makes things appear larger or more important than they really are. In journalism, too often, the aim is to gobsmack people beyond what the facts warrant, especially on the weekend TV news services.

I once worked in a newsroom where the journos, for a laugh, presented each other with an Iron Bar Award for the biggest beat-up of the week. A real iron bar, it was not something anyone really wanted to win, an object of derision not desire. The boss, missing the point, confiscated it.

The bar had served as a reminder that gross exaggeration created a distorted sense of perspective. If the earth was 'huge', for example, how large was Jupiter and how big was the universe? Very, very, very huge?

Personally, having grown older and less excitable these days, I prefer it when the facts are left to speak for themselves. The unadorned truth is usually remarkable enough.

Some exaggerations are harmless. The Big Lobster. The Big Orange. We all exaggerate the weather – it is so hot, the chickens are laying hard-boiled eggs – or the size of the fish that got away or our sex lives.

But in none of these areas do we really expect to be taken seriously, a bit like telling someone: I want your honest feedback. Sure.

Thanks to the Food & Wine silliness, poor old Ying Chow will now have to live with the burden of being called the best. Even the advertising industry, for whom everything is new, improved or better, would not have dared use such an exaggerated superlative.

Should any of F&W's US readers bother to journey to the other side of the planet to dine at the best Chinese restaurant in the universe, I suggest they bring ear plugs.

If nothing else, Ying Chow is LOUD and NOISY. I cannot hear myself talk in there and that's no exaggeration.

22 January 2003

Secret men's room business exposed

Fellow traveller Richard B. worries a lot and George W. Bush is his current major worry, with good reason, as he reflects gloomily on the world's impending doom.

His starting point for argument's sake is 250 million Americans own 50 per cent of the world's wealth with no apparent intention of sharing it, and bad things shall come to pass as a consequence.

Richard, a benign man in all other respects, has a rather perverse sense of humour that makes him good entertainment at lunch over a bottle of wine, as we were doing the other day in the company of an older woman.

Into the second bottle, it happened that Richard and I made a move for the toilet at the same time.

We hesitated – 'You go first.' ... 'No, you.' ... 'No, I insist' – and our female guest wondered why we did not just go together?

Yes, were we women, we absolutely would have insisted on going together. Apart from having someone else check if the back of your dress is tucked into your knickers, I can think of no explanation.

Anyway, my need was more pressing than Richard's at the time and I went first, making the excuse that we could not let the lady sit by herself even though she seemed perfectly content with her wine and duck.

Richard waited to take his turn and when we had all settled down again, he asked why straight mates never went to the toilet together if they could help it and, if they did, why they stood as far away from one another as possible?

Richard happens to be gay and I am not, so our experiences in public toilets may be somewhat different.

He had other questions, too: Who is the more butch, the guy who leaves first or the guy who takes longest? Do real men wash their hands? Do all stockmen describe the ABC symbol in the dust?

Which reminded me of an old joke about the man coming home late and relieving himself in the snow in his front yard. Chastised by his wife next morning, he indignantly denied it until she said: 'I recognised your hand writing.'

Richard then revealed that he suffered from what he called nervous bladder syndrome whenever he went to a 'straight' toilet.

He said he would stand at the ready but nothing happened if someone else was present. He worried that standing there doing nothing might look a bit sus' to the other guy.

But fleeing the scene only meant he had to go again soon, which made it look like he was going too often – even more sus'.

Richard therefore preferred the privacy of a cubicle.

I told him I had not given these weighty matters much thought and now was secretly dreading having to go again myself within the next half hour.

Meantime, I asked Richard, given his leftish geopolitical viewpoint, if he thought John Howard and George W. went to the toilet together?

Definitely, he said, and probably stood close enough to hold hands.

29 January 2003

Index of headlines

Wakefield Press is an independent publishing and
distribution company based in Adelaide, South Australia.
We love good stories and publish beautiful books.
To see our full range of titles, please visit our website at
www.wakefieldpress.com.au.

Wakefield Press thanks Fox Creek Wines
and Arts South Australia for their support.